SECURE and RESILIENT SOFTWARE

Requirements, Test Cases, and Testing Methods

SECURE and RESILIENT SOFTWARE

Requirements, Test Cases, and Testing Methods

Mark S. Merkow and Lakshmikanth Raghavan

CRC Press
Taylor & Francis Group
Boca Raton London New York

CRC Press is an imprint of the
Taylor & Francis Group, an **informa** business

AN AUERBACH BOOK

CRC Press
Taylor & Francis Group
6000 Broken Sound Parkway NW, Suite 300
Boca Raton, FL 33487-2742

© 2012 by Taylor & Francis Group, LLC
CRC Press is an imprint of Taylor & Francis Group, an Informa business

No claim to original U.S. Government works

Version Date: 20111005

International Standard Book Number: 978-1-4398-6621-4 (Hardback)

Library of Congress Cataloging-in-Publication Data

Merkow, Mark S.
    Secure and resilient software : requirements, test cases, and testing methods / Mark S. Merkow, Lakshmikanth Raghavan.
        p. cm.
    Includes bibliographical references and index.
    ISBN 978-1-4398-6621-4 (hardcover : alk. paper)
    1. Computer software--Testing. 2. Computer software--Reliability. 3. Computer security. 4. Application software--Development. I. Raghavan, Lakshmikanth. II. Title.

QA76.76.T48M47 2012
005.8--dc23   2011036908

Visit the Taylor & Francis Web site at
http://www.taylorandfrancis.com

and the CRC Press Web site at
http://www.crcpress.com

Contents

Preface

Systems Analysis Paralysis has met its doom!

With the tools and techniques from this book, you'll find it's worth its weight in gold! We've done the heavy lifting for you in compiling a comprehensive set of software requirements for security, resilience, and any of the other "-ilities" you can dream up, freeing you to concentrate on improving software and its development without being stuck in the quicksand of analysis and design delays.

As a companion to our book, *Secure and Resilient Software Development* (CRC Press, 2010), we've focused the attention of this book on the earliest phases of the software development lifecycle (SDLC), making accessible to you useful and proven techniques that, when properly applied, can only serve to produce high-quality and easy-to-maintain applications that will make you the envy of your peers! *Security and Resilience Software Requirements, Test Cases, and Testing Methods* gives you ground-level, directly usable software nonfunctional requirements and corresponding test cases and methods for conducting those tests to help assure your development team's ability to quickly incorporate nonfunctional requirements into system specifications and assure that those requirements will show up in developed systems.

Because catching errors when they are introduced can save you a up to a hundred times the cost that would be incurred if the flaw migrated into the final application, this book is intended to help you trap those errors before they become flaws and eliminate them for good. Improving the SDLC itself is as much a goal and outcome as improving the applications that it produces, and you have in your hands everything you need to specify good programs, make sure they're developed with goodness intact, and test cases and test methods to ensure that little if anything gets past the layers of a defensive SDLC.

Security and Resilience Software Requirements, Test Cases, and Testing Methods was written with the following people in mind:

- Application/applet developers
- Software designers
- Web application systems analysts
- Software support personnel
- Payment card industry payment application (PA) standard and data security standard (DSS) auditors
- Security architects
- Enterprise architects
- Application development department managers
- IT security professionals and consultants
- Project managers
- Application software security professionals
- Instructors and trainers for secure application development techniques and practices

How This Book Is Organized

Chapter 1 opens the book with a contextual understanding of what secure and resilient applications are, and discusses design flaws that lead to serious vulnerabilities and consequences and the ways that defects increase the costs of software maintenance and support.

Chapter 2 reviews the characteristics of high-quality software, expands on the concepts of nonfunctional requirements, and introduces the System Quality Requirements Engineering (SQUARE) Methodology from Carnegie-Mellon University. Chapter 3 begins peeling the onion of nonfunctional requirements and their considerations as they relate to the quality of applications and its runtime environment.

Chapter 4, the heart of the book, describes 93 software assurance functional requirements for you to use in your own specifications, relieving you of the painstaking effort of defining and documenting these requirements from scratch.

Chapter 5 moves into describing how security is implemented as series of policy-enforcing services that applications should use through standardized APIs. Chapter 6 moves into the design phase of the SDLC by providing comprehensive recommendations and considerations for converting requirements into positive steps that help to ensure that software is designed securely, developed securely, and operated securely. Chapter 7 then goes into the next level of detail for converting requirements into application design choices.

Chapter 8 moves into the testing phase of the SDLC by providing you test cases that are related to the security requirements we provided in Chapter 4. These test cases are intended for you to use when developing a testing plan, which is then used for comprehensive testing of both the application's functional requirements and its security requirements.

Chapter 9 offers you some tools and best practices for testing application software for assurance that security features are present and working as intended in candidate release applications. It provides an inside look at the OWASP Application Security Verification Standard (ASVS) for normalizing the range of coverage and level of rigor for performing Web application security verification. Chapter 10 then wraps up the book with a framework and roadmap to help you implement what you learned in Chapters 1 through 9.

For updates to this book and ongoing activities of interest to the secure and resilient software community, please visit www.srsdlc.com.

What's On the CD?

The enclosed CD contains electronic versions of several of the documents and templates referenced in Secure and Resilient Software: Requirements, Test Cases, and Testing Methods

On the CD you will find:
- 93 security requirements from Chapter 4 as MS Word files
- 73 test Cases from Chapter 8 as MS Word files for testing the requirements selected
- Checklists from Chapters 3 and 6

Requirements

In the **RequirementTemplates** folder on the CD you will find the 93 requirements organized by the security topics they reference. Each requirement family has its own directory and within each directory are separate MS Word template files along with a Directory file that contains the requirement file name and its description:

- Identification Requirements – Folder IDEN
- Authentication Requirements – Folder ATEN
- Authorization Requirements – Folder AUTR
- Security Auditing Requirements – Folder AUDT
- Confidentiality Requirements – Folder CONF
- Integrity Requirements – Folder INTG
- Availability Requirements – Folder AVAL
- Non-repudiation Requirements – Folder NREP
- Immunity Requirements – Folder IMMU
- Survivability Requirements – Folder SURV
- Systems Maintenance Requirements – Folder SYSM
- Privacy Requirements – Folder PRIV

You can use these requirements in any number of ways:

- Export them in any file format that MS Word supports into your Requirements Management System
- Copy and update them for your Business Requirements Document (BRD), Master Requirements Document (MRD, or whatever you use to specify system functional and nonfunctional requirements)

Test Cases

In the **TestCasesTemplates** folder on the CD you will find the 73 test cases and a directory for them. Each test case supports one of more security requirements from Chapter 4.

Using the Test Cases

You can use the test case templates to create your customized testing plans for your software based on the techniques described in Chapter 10. These test cases can be combined and integrated into your own test plan document and imported into your testing platform (if it is supported).

Checklists

In the Checklists folder on the CD you will find electronic versions of:

- Table 3.3   Requirements Gathering Phase Completion Checklist
- Table 6.4   MSDN Architecture and Design Review Checklist

About the Authors

Mark S. Merkow, CISSP, CISM, CSSLP works at PayPal Inc. (an eBay company) in Scottsdale, Arizona, as Manager of Information Security Policies, Standards, Training, and Awareness in the Information Risk Management area. Mark has more than 35 years of experience in information technology in a variety of roles, including applications development, systems analysis and design, security engineering, and security management. Mark holds a masters degree in decision and info systems from Arizona State University (ASU), a masters of education in distance learning from ASU, and an undergraduate degree in computer info systems from ASU. In addition to his day job, Mark engages in a number of other extracurricular activities, including consulting, course development, online course delivery, and writing columns and books on information technology and information security.

Mark has authored or coauthored ten books on IT and is a contributing editor on four others.

Mark remains very active within the information security community, working in a variety of roles for the Financial Services Information Sharing and Analysis Center (FS-ISAC), the Financial Services Technology Consortium (FSTC), and the Financial Services Sector Coordinating Council (FSCCC) on Homeland Security and Critical Infrastructure Protection. He is the chairman of the Education Committee for the FS-ISAC and is a founding member of the Research and Development Committee of the FSSCC.

Lakshmikanth Raghavan, CISM, CRISC (Laksh) works at PayPal Inc. (an eBay company) as Staff Information Security Engineer in the Information Risk Management area, specializing in application security. Laksh has more than ten years of experience in the areas of information security and information risk management, and has provided consulting services to Fortune 500 companies and financial services companies around the world.

Laksh holds a bachelor's degree in electronics and telecommunication engineering from the University of Madras, India. He enjoys writing security-related articles and has spoken on the various dimensions of software security at industry forums and security conferences.

This is Laksh's second book.

Acknowledgements

From Mark Merkow

To start, I'm thankful to my friend and co-author, Laksh Raghavan, who apparently was born with the mission to improve the state of software quality and the skill to share his depth of knowledge and expertise with the rest of the planet!

Thanks to my wife, Amy, and to my family for the ongoing support and encouragement in my writing another book.

The following people deserve appreciation beyond measure for their help, support, expertise, encouragement, and reassurance, which make the process of writing far easier than it otherwise is: Gus Anagnos, Denise Anderson, Mark Ardis, Robert Auger, Warren Axelrod, Michael Barrett, Doug Cavit, John Carlson, Joseph Cavanaugh, Don Cochran, Cindy Donaldson, Jeff Edelen, Chris Faciana, Beth Hubbard, Ajoy Kumar, Wally Lake, James Landis, Doug Maughan, Nancy Mead, Bill Nelson, Jim Palmer, Brian Peretti, David Rice, Robert Rodriguez, Jim Routh, Dan Schutzer, Paul Smocer, Andy Steingruebl, Nicole Stuchlik, Roger Thornton, Jeff Weekes, Angela Weinman, Errol Weiss, Jeff Williams and Leigh Williams.

Tremendous thanks goes to Theron Shreve, John Wyzalek, and the entire staff at Derryfield Publishing Services and Taylor and Francis for their commitment to excellence, efficiency, humor, and drive that makes working with them a total pleasure!

Special thanks goes to my agent, Carole McClendon, and the crew at Waterside Productions.

From Laksh Raghavan

First up, I'm truly indebted to my mentor and coauthor, Mark Merkow, for providing me one more opportunity to be part of a book project. But for his timely, invaluable inputs and continuous guidance, this book wouldn't have been possible.

Thanks to my wife, Janani, for her encouragement and continued support for another book project. Heartfelt thanks to my parents and my family for their overwhelming encouragement.

A million thanks and deepest gratitude to the following people who have enlightened me with their expertise and encouraged me with their warm words: Gus Anagnos, Robert Auger, Warren Axelrod, Michael Barrett, Bhaskar Bhattacharya, Joseph Cavanaugh, Bil Corry, Avinandan Datta, Jeff Edelen, Kevin Glass, Ryan Gurney, Sanjeev Harit, Jeff Hodges, Madhukar I.B., Ashish Kumar, Santhosh Kumar, Wally Lake, James Landis, Upendra Mardikar, Rick Marvin, Brett McDowell, Debarshi Mukherjee, Chandar N, Rohit Nand, Jim Palmer, Pierre Pellissier, Sneha Phadke, Robert Raja, Ram Ramdattan, Srini Rangaraj, Srikar Sagi, Arun Selvarajan, Kurihara Shinji, Adam Shostack, Nittono Shuuji, Andy Steingruebl, Piramanayagam T, Alex Tosheff, Murali V, David Weisman, Jeff Williams and Nam Wu.

Special thanks to John Wyzalek, Theron Shreve and the entire production crew at Derryfield Publishing Services and Taylor and Francis for their professional support & guidance in getting this book done.

Tremendous thanks to my agent, Carole McClendon, and the crew at Waterside Productions—for always getting stuff done at warp speed!

Chapter 1

Introduction

Economic costs of faulty software in the United States range in the tens of billions of dollars every year and represent about one percent of the U.S. gross domestic product (GDP).[1]

And things are getting worse.

In efforts to "do something" about the problem, we've gone from ignoring it, to acknowledging its existence, and lately to testing for vulnerabilities that we're certain we'll find. Rather than trying to test-in quality, would it not be better to *build it in* from the start?

Secure and resilient application software can only emerge from a software development lifecycle (SDLC) that treats nonfunctional requirements (NFRs) and quality requirements as a *core element of every phase*, as well as in postdeployment. By mandating security and resilience within the SDLC itself and ensuring that requirements related to security and resilience are treated as *equal citizens* with all functional requirements, managers can rest better at night knowing their infrastructure and applications are continuously working as their defender rather than their enemy.

In our book entitled *Secure and Resilient Software Development*,[2] we advocated an environment in which software security and resilience require a holistic, comprehensive approach. The primary goal of this book is to help people understand that when NFRs are neglected at program specification time, they will not magically appear when the application undergoes testing.

Failing to specify any desirable quality features up front is a surefire recipe for guaranteeing their absence!

1.1 Secure and Resilient

In *Secure and Resilient Software Development*, we defined software resilience as:

> *. . . the ability to reduce the magnitude and/or duration of disruptive events. The effectiveness of a resilient application or infrastructure software depends on its ability to anticipate, absorb, adapt to, and/or recover rapidly from a potentially disruptive event.*
> *(Secure and Resilient Software Development, Chapter 1, p. 2)*

Resilient and secure code is neither cheap nor easy to attain, but unless it's thoroughly considered from the start of a development project till the very end, it's completely unattainable. Bolting on security to an insecurely developed application will *not* make it secure or resilient—it will only make it more complicated to understand, maintain, and operate.

Testing for security features and testing for security bugs in the later phases of the SDLC while ignoring security and resilience NFRs in all earlier SDLC phases will not produce a secure and resilient application. Just as quality cannot be tested in to products, high-quality application development requires stringent attention from the very start.

A common recurring theme in software development shops is the difficulty in specifying what's needed at the start of a development effort for security and resilience. This book is intended to help reduce this difficulty and help systems analysts, designers, and would-be users of the application to document these NFRs by reusing and customizing what we offer here.

1.2   Bad Design Choices Led to the Vulnerable Internet We Know Today

In a presentation entitled "Internet Nails," Marcus Ranum presents[3] a detailed recap of small, yet bad, design choices made by well-meaning engineers long ago that resulted in significant downstream problems with the technologies that run the Internet today.

One example is the file transfer protocol (FTP), which was developed around 1971. FTP was used to transfer files from one computer to another during the early ARPANET days, long before the commercial Internet came into being. A few years later, another protocol called "host-to-host protocol" was developed, then later renamed as network control protocol (NCP). NCP was then reimplemented and rewritten by software engineers as the transmission control protocol (TCP)—the underlying technology that runs the Internet today.

To understand the issues of TCP requires an understanding of network sockets. In simple terms, network sockets are abstract rendezvous points for two systems to use for communicating over the Internet. All connections on the Internet happen using network sockets in a simple four-step process:

1. A server listens for traffic on particular socket port.

2. A client connects to that port on the server.

3. The client transmits its data.

4. Once the data transmission is complete, the client disconnects.

With FTP, it's a little more complicated. Figure 1.1 and the list below show the steps required for using the FTP protocol:

1. The FTP server listens on particular network socket port.

2. A client connects to that port on the server and transmits USER login command to the server.

3. The server responds with a request for the "Password".

4. The client sends the user's password to the server.

5. When the client requests a file it *creates and listens* to a port chosen at random and sends *a message back* to the server instructing it to "transfer the file to the port that it just created and on which it is actively listening."

6. The server then *connects back to the client* on that port and transmits the file.

7. The client then drops the connection to the server with a "Bye".

Take a look at steps 5 and 6 in the list. Does it seem odd to you that the protocol specifies having the client open the port and having the server connect back to it? When the host-to-host protocol was written, data could only be transmitted in one direction over a socket, and the same was true with NCP. Once TCP/IP was developed, this problem was solved and data could travel in both directions on a socket, but FTP was never rewritten to take advantage of that feature.

FTP continued to work the way it always did, and no one thought to redesign it. So why does this matter in the long run?

The unexpected effect was that FTP inadvertently created the need for a firewall! In the early days of TCP/IP, existing router technologies could not

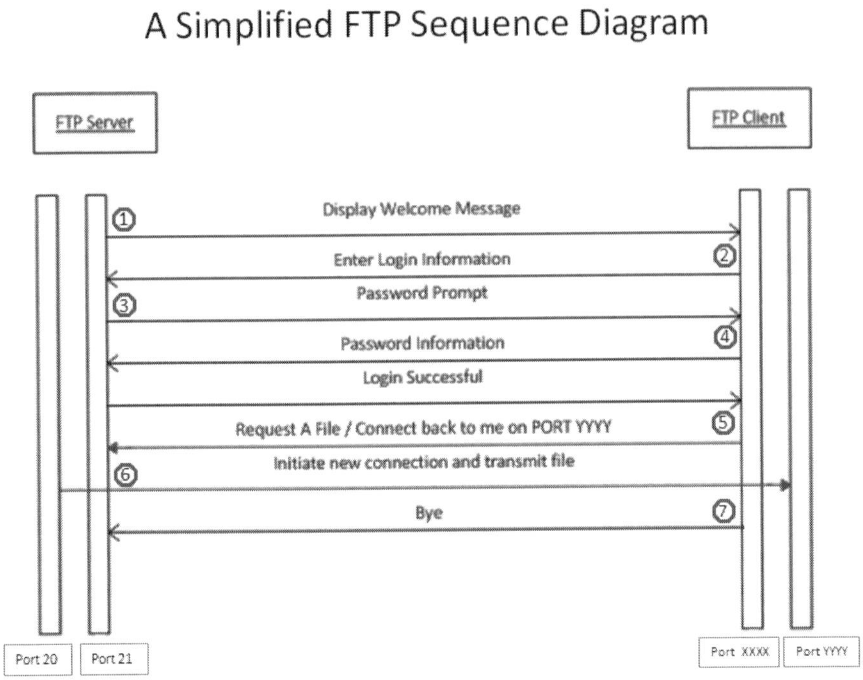

A Simplified FTP Sequence Diagram

Figure 1.1   A Simplified FTP Sequence Diagram

handle the odd "callback" behavior of FTP (steps 7 and 8) because corporations wanted to control and prevent random people the outside from connecting back into their networks.

Engineers, including Marcus Ranum, began developing firewall systems. In 1991, Ranum sold his first firewall for $195,000. This firewall industry grew into a $100 million industry by 1997; by 2009, network edge defense technology (with firewalls that added more and more functions like spam filtering) was estimated to be a billion-dollar industry!

In hindsight, it would have taken a couple of hours for a good programmer to fix FTP back in 1975. Since then, the industry has spent millions of dollars on this problem, and making it worse still—FTP remains in use with the same problems!

1.3   HTTP Has Its Problems, Too

Let's now take a look at some of the design choices made on the hypertext transfer protocol (HTTP) and the downstream consequences that we continue dealing with today.

In the early 1990s, the Internet implementation was largely dominated by the Berkeley System Distribution (BSD) UNIX operating system and its derivatives. The TCP/IP stack across all these UNIX versions used the same codebase. In that TCP/IP implementation, there was a concept of *incoming connection limit*. The protocol specifies a partial socket table and a system socket table. Since the programmers of the stack had very little program and system memory (~1 MB) to use, they made a choice to have twelve entries for the partial socket table and 2048 entries for the system socket table. Whenever a new incoming connection was initiated, one of the twelve entries in the partial table would be filled. TCP is a stateful protocol and requires a *three-way handshake* to fully set it up. Until such time that the handshake completes, the entry is queued up in the partial table. Once the connection is fully set up, the entry is removed and moved to the system socket table.

After a time, some of these UNIX systems began crashing when thirteen partial connections were made to them—the OS didn't know how to deal with more than twelve, as the protocol stack had a limitation of just twelve.

Around 1995, Sir Tim Berners-Lee developed the World Wide Web (WWW), and because of this overloaded socket problem, he decided to make HTTP stateless—meaning there would be no continuity between request and response pairs. A Web page might trigger five, ten, or even fifteen different connections, depending on the contents of the page and the browser would then assemble all of these objects into a single formatted web page.

Making such separate requests one-by-one (serially) would cause a page to load very slowly. In response, browser programmers implemented some performance hacks—they loaded all of those images and objects in four or five *parallel* connections, rather than serially. Servers then were handed a hard problem of dealing with five parallel connections instead of just one from a single client.

To fix this problem, by 1996, the UNIX server programmers changed their code so that the server could handle tens of thousands of incoming connections at a time.

In 1997, after Internet commerce took off, people noticed that HTTP, being a stateless protocol, was not so great after all, for various reasons:

- *Security*: A developer had to encrypt all the confidential data between the server and client, and all keys negotiated for the encryption had to be discarded after that stateless connection was closed, which is computationally expensive.

- *Shopping carts*: When a user added an item to their shopping cart and navigated away from that page for other items, the cart would be empty.
- *Logging in and tracking*: There were issues with Web site logins and with keeping track of what a user does on a site once they're logged in.

To solve this problem, a separate session management scheme had to be implemented. Cookies were designed and developed to enable servers to maintain the state of a Web session. Several problems showed up right away:

- Software frameworks such as PHP, .NET, AJAX, Ruby, and others each had to support new models to reintroduce state management in the form of *session management*. Each of those frameworks did this in their own way, and programmers had to learn what each technology required for correct implementation.
- Load balancers had to be put in front of Web server farms to track state for each Web connection
- New vulnerabilities, like session hijacking, cross-site scripting, SQL injection attacks, and others were made possible because of these new implementations.

1.4   Design Errors Continue Haunting Us Today

Today we still are dealing with some bad design choices that were made earlier. Eric Butler, a freelance Web application developer, released[4] FireSheep. This Firefox browser plug-in lets anyone on an open wireless network sniff out (copy) other users' cookies that are intended for sites that only use SSL for the login process but not for the rest of the session (Hotmail is a good example of this). When logging into a Web site, you begin by submitting your username and password. The server then checks to see if an account matching this information exists and, if it does, replies back to your browser with a *cookie* used by your browser for all subsequent requests to that site. It's extremely common for Web sites to protect your password by encrypting the initial login, but very uncommon for them to encrypt all other traffic. This leaves the cookie and the user it belongs to vulnerable. On an open wireless network, cookies are basically broadcast through the air, making these attacks extremely easy to pull off.

Looking back, the fundamental problem that led to the "stateless" design choice for HTTP was already fixed by 1996, before the World Wide Web and e-commerce became mainstream—but nobody went back and redesigned HTTP . . .

In their report *2010 Top Cyber Security Risks,*, HP Digital Vaccine Labs details a sharp rise in attacks in 2010 targeting Web applications. They claim this is due to botnet-based attack toolkits that exploit known Web application vulnerabilities to compromise user machines and company servers. "There's a growing market of underground, mafia-type organizations that develop and maintain toolkits for helping criminals compromise and monetize victims . . . We're seeing specialized scripts that you can load onto a host after you've compromised it that will use the host to launch further attacks, and that script may only be 100 Kbytes in length," said Mike Dausin, manager of advanced security intelligence for HP DVLabs.[5]

1.5   Requirements & Design: The Keys to a Successful Software Project

In an *IEEE Spectrum Magazine* article,[6] Robert Charter explains some of the common reasons software projects fail. The article covers a variety of pitfalls, ranging from "unrealistic or unarticulated project goals" to "poor project management,." Two of the pernicious reasons actually lie within the software development lifecycle itself:

- Badly defined system requirements
- Sloppy development practices

The article explains how critical requirements are within the SDLC. Consider a purchasing system that automates the ordering, billing, and shipping of parts. A salesperson can input a customer's order, have it automatically check the pricing and contract requirements, and arrange to have the parts and invoice sent to the customer from the warehouse.

The requirements for the system specify four basic steps.

1. The sales process creates a bill of sale.
2. The bill of sale is sent through a legal review process for the contractual terms and conditions of the potential sale and approves them.
3. The provisioning process sends out the parts purchased.
4. The finance process sends out an invoice.

Without clear requirements for Step 1, programmers may treat every order as though it was placed in the company's main location, even though the company has branches in several states and countries. That single mistake, in turn, affects how tax is calculated, what kind of contract is issued, what shipping rates are used, and so on.

The sooner the error is detected and corrected, the better. Think about knitting a sweater. If you spot a missed stitch right after you make it, you can simply unravel a bit of yarn, correct the mistake, and move on. But if you don't catch the mistake until the end, you may need to ravel all the way back to that stitch just to redo it.

If the software development team fails to catch their omission until final system testing—or worse, after the system has been rolled out—the costs to correct the error are many times greater than if they'd caught the mistake while they were still working on the initial sales process program.

Unlike a missed stitch in a sweater, the problem is far harder to pinpoint—the programmers only see that errors are appearing, but do not know which of several causes might be in play. Even after the original error is corrected, the programmers will need to change all other calculations and documentation and then retest every step.

From the earliest days of software development, studies have shown that the cost of remediating vulnerabilities or flaws in design are far lower when they're caught and fixed during the early requirements/design phases than after launching the software into production.

Figure 1.2 shows the phases of the SDLC in which defects are introduced; seventy percent of them are introduced in the Requirements and Design phases. However, detecting the majority of those defects does not happen until the user acceptance testing phase or after the application goes into production.

Barry Boehm blames[7] late inspection for software errors as the cause of an increase of up to one hundred times the cost that would have been required if the errors were caught sooner in the SDLC, as illustrated in Figure 1.3. If a defect is found in the earlier SDLC phases, costs to remove it or prevent it are minimal. If the defect is not found until after the software is launched and placed in maintenance mode, the cost to remediate it is one hundred times more.[8]

Therefore, the earlier you can integrate security processes into the development life cycle, the cheaper software development becomes over the long haul.

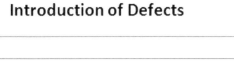

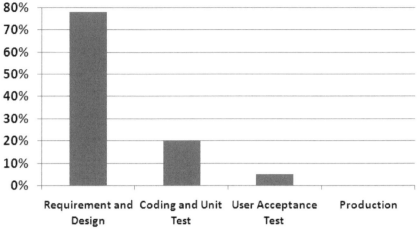

Figure 1.2   SDLC Phases in Which Defects Are Introduced

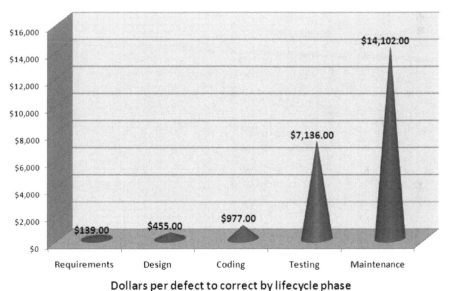

Dollars per defect to correct by lifecycle phase

Figure 1.3   Costs of Fixing Errors by Phase

1.6   How Design Flaws Play Out

Following are some examples of what can happen when design flaws make their way into production systems, devices, and products that are intended for the public's use.

1.6.1   DNS Vulnerability

In early 2008, Dan Kaminsky discovered a critical vulnerability in the domain name service (DNS) system. The DNS system translates domain names that people understand, like www.blah.com, to IP addresses that computers understand, like 204.11.200.1. This creates an entire family of vulnerabilities—for example, the DNS system on PCs can be fooled into thinking that the IP address for www.badsite.com is really the IP address for www.goodsite.com, and there's no way for users to tell the difference. This flaw allows the criminals at www.badsite.com to trick you into doing all sorts of things when your browser takes you to their site, like giving up your bank account details. Kaminsky had discovered a particularly nasty variant of this DNS cache-poisoning attack.

What's important is how *good design decisions* can make software secure and resilient from vulnerabilities and attacks yet to come. Years ago, cryptographer Daniel J. Bernstein looked at DNS security and decided that source port randomization was a smart design choice. Bernstein didn't know about Kaminsky's attack, but he saw a general class of attacks and realized that this enhancement could protect against them. Consequently, the DNS program he wrote in 2000, "djbdns", did not need to be patched—it was already immune to Kaminsky's attack. That's what a good design looks like. It's not just secure against known attacks; it's also secure against unknown attacks and attacks yet to come.

1.6.2   The London Stock Exchange

Back in 1986, the London Stock Exchange decided[9] to automate its system for settling stock transactions. Seven years later, after spending $600 million, it scrapped the Taurus system's development, not only because the design was excessively complex and cumbersome, but also because the management of the project was, in the words of one of its own senior managers, "delusional." As investigations revealed, no one wanted to know the true status of the project, even as problems stacked up, deadlines were missed, and costs soared.

1.6.3   Medical Equipment

Medical equipment is not immune to bad software either. In a series of accidents, therapy planning software created by Multidata Systems International, a U.S. firm, miscalculated[10] the proper dosage of radiation for patients undergoing radiation therapy. Multidata's software allowed a radiation therapist to draw on a computer screen the placement of metal shields called "blocks" designed to protect healthy tissue from the radiation.

However, the software only allowed technicians to use four shielding blocks. Doctors in Panama wanted to use five! The doctors discovered that they could trick the software by drawing all five blocks as a single large block with a hole in the middle. What the doctors did not realize is that the Multidata software computed different answers in the configuration depending on how the hole was drawn—draw it in one direction and the correct dose is calculated, draw it in another direction and the software recommends twice the necessary exposure of radiation.

A subsequent International Atomic Energy Agency (IAEA) report stated[11] that there were several characteristics of the computerized treatment planning system that made it relatively easy for the error to occur. These were:

1. Differing ways of digitizing blocks were accepted by the computer treatment planning system.

2. There was no warning on the computer screen when blocks were digitized in an unacceptable way (i.e., any way that was different from the one prescribed in the manual).

3. When blocks were digitized incorrectly, the treatment planning system still produced a diagram that was the same as those produced when the data was entered correctly, thereby giving the impression that the calculated results were correct.

At least eight patients died, while another twenty received overdoses likely to cause significant health problems. The Panamanian physicians, who were legally required to double-check the computer's calculations by hand, were indicted for murder.

1.6.4   Airbus A380

The Airbus A380, the largest passenger airliner in the world, was also bitten by bad software. In a Pan-European project[12] to build the world's biggest passenger plane, you might expect the language barriers between management and engineers, but you'd hope the computers at least would speak the same language.

In the spring of 2005, however, just as the Airbus A380 was taking shape in hangars outside Toulouse, France, engineers came across a huge software issue that reportedly cost the company $6 billion by delaying the first flight by two years.

The French production facility had been using the latest version of the industry standard computer-aided design (CAD) software, CATIA 5, for its CAD designs. The Germans, on the other hand, had worked in CATIA 4, which handles 3D objects differently.

When they tried to match up their halves of the plane, it was like trying to weld the front of a Chevrolet Camaro to the back of a Cadillac Escalade. The biggest problem was that the wiring plans were completely incompatible. Subtle differences in the software meant mismatched connections needed rerouting to connect the two disparate halves of the plane.

Even when developers wrote code to translate between the two versions, complications remained, with engineers pointing out that there was insufficient space to carry power cables far enough away from signal wires to prevent interference.

If you're wiring one plug, a couple of late changes to a wiring diagram isn't a major issue, but with the A380's 530 km of cabling, more than 100,000 individual wires, and 40,000 connectors, a single change has a negative cascading effect.

The list of problems could go on and on to fill all the pages of this book. But, what we're looking for are solutions that every software designer, developer, architect, and tester can use to make their own software secure and resilient.

1.7   Solutions Are In Sight!

Software security is one of those legacy problems that will not be solved overnight. It requires a substantial investment in the right tools and processes, active diligence, ongoing awareness and evangelism, continuing education, and determination to make any headway.

Organizations need a set of well-defined, reusable requirements for security and resilience in order to bootstrap secure software development efforts. Developing a set of security requirements is a fundamental foundational step in the SDLC. Testers need those requirements to build their test cases. With no documented requirements, there would be no test cases and no assurance whatsoever that NFRs would make it into software that the public will use—and letting malicious users become your security testers is a great strategy for failure, or worse!

Organizations that develop software also need robust sets of test cases and testing methods to ensure that those requirements have been properly implemented in the software being developed.

In upcoming chapters we'll provide exhaustive detailed requirements, test cases, and testing methods to help you make sure that you're incorporating the right kind of nonfunctional requirements in the right place and the right time for all your software development projects.

1.8 Notes

1. "The Economic Impacts of Inadequate Infrastructure for Software Testing," National Institute of Standards & Technology, accessed March 10, 2011, www.nist.gov/director/planning/upload/report02-3.pdf.

2. Mark S. Merkow & Lakshmikanth Raghavan, *Secure and Resilient Software Development* (CRC Press, 2010).

3. "TEDxMidAtlantic: Marcus Ranum," YouTube, accessed December 19, 2010, www.youtube.com/watch?v=o59mQhBiUo4.

4. "Firesheep," codebutler [blog], accessed November 17, 2010, http://codebutler.com/firesheep.

5. "Web Applications See Sharp Rise In Attacks," *Information Week*, accessed April 12, 2011, www.informationweek.com/news/security/vulnerabilities/   showArticle.jhtml?articleID=229400808&cid=RSSfeed_IWK_News,
    and
    "Reducing Risk through Requirements-Driven Quality Management: An End-to-End Approach," HP Software Customer Connection, accessed April 11, 2011, http://viewer.media.bitpipe.com/1000733242_857/1181846419_126/74536mg.pdf.

6. "Why Software Fails," *IEEE Spectrum: Technology, Engineering, and Science News*, accessed December 18, 2010, http://spectrum.ieee.org/computing/software/why-software-fails/0.

7. Barry W. Boehm and Richard Turner, *Balancing Agility and Discipline: A Guide for the Perplexed* (Boston, MA: Addison-Wesley, 2006).

8. Barry W. Boehm and V. Basili, "Software Defect Reduction Top 10 List," *IEEE Computer* (IEEE Computer Society, Vol. 34, No. 1, January 2001.)

9. "Why Software Fails," *IEEE Spectrum: Technology, Engineering, and Science News*, accessed December 18, 2010http://spectrum.ieee.org/computing/software/why-software-fails/4.

10. "History's Worst Software Bugs," *Wired*, accessed December 19, 2010, www.wired.com/software/coolapps/news/2005/11/69355?currentPage=all.

11. "NRC Information Notice 2001-08, Supplement 2: Update On Radiation Therapy Overexposures In Panama," Massachusetts Insitute of Technology, accessed December 19, 2010, http://web.mit.edu/6.033/www/papers/theratron.pdf.

12. "When Computers Go Wrong," *PC Pro*, accessed December 19, 2010, www.pcpro.co.uk/features/363580/when-computers-go-wrong/5.

Chapter 2

Nonfunctional Requirements (NFRs) in Context

Throughout this book, we have bound security and resilience together because, in many cases, when you're using a *defensive software development methodology* to meet security objectives, resilience tags along for the ride. Examples include improved reliability, rapid recoverability, and simplified portability. Other NFRs require deliberate attention and relate to both the application itself and the environment under which your applications run.

Keep in mind the following working definition of nonfunctional requirements as you proceed through the book:

> *NFR: A software requirement that describes not what the software will do but how the software will do it-for example, software performance requirements, software external interface requirements, software design constraints, and software quality attributes.*[1]

In Chapter 2, you will learn about the model for System Quality Requirements Engineering (SQUARE) as well as what constitutes a good requirement description.

2.1 System Quality Requirements Engineering (SQUARE)

System Quality Requirements Engineering (SQUARE) is a process model developed[2] at Carnegie Mellon University (CMU). SQUARE provides a means for eliciting, categorizing, and prioritizing security requirements for information technology systems and applications. The focus of the model is to build security and quality concepts into the early stages of the development life cycle. The model can also be used for documenting and analyzing the security and quality aspects of a development project.

The nine different steps of SQUARE are:

1.   Agree on definitions
2.   Identify security goals
3.   Develop artifacts to support security requirements definition
4.   Assess risks
5.   Select elicitation technique(s)
6.   Elicit security requirements
7.   Categorize requirements
8.   Prioritize requirements
9.   Inspect requirements

SQUARE usually requires about three months of effort to complete. CMU also developed a shorter version, called *SQUARE-Lite*, with these five steps:

1.   Agree on definitions
2.   Identify assets and security goals
3.   Perform risk assessment
4.   Elicit security requirements
5.   Prioritize requirements

SQUARE-Lite can be used by organizations that already have a requirements engineering process in place and want to fit security and quality requirements into it, or by organizations that have not yet decided to implement the full SQUARE process model but still want some of the benefits. Let's look at these five steps in detail.

2.1.1   Agree on Definitions

Agreement is the initial step that the requirements engineering team and stakeholders undergo. They must first agree on a common set of terminology and definitions. The process is carried out through a set of interviews and guarantees effective and clear communication throughout the requirements engineering process. This involves using public resources, such as the Software Engineering Body of Knowledge (SWEBOK) [IEEE 05], the IEEE 610.12 Standard Glossary of Software Engineering Terminology [IEEE 90], and Wikipedia.

Agreement also resolves ambiguity and differences in perspective. The exit criteria for this step are a documented set of definitions. Typical examples are access control (ACL), antivirus software, artifacts, assets, control, attacks, audit information, authentication, availability, back doors, breaches, brute force, buffer overflow, cache cramming, cache poisoning, confidentiality, nonrepudiation, denial-of-service (DoS), intrusion, malware, and so on.

2.1.2   Identify Assets and Security/Quality Goals

Identifying assets that need protection in the system and their corresponding security and quality goals is the next objective. Initially, different stakeholders will have different security and quality goals. Development teams need to formally agree on a set of prioritized security goals for the project. Without overall security goals for the project, it is impossible to identify the priority and relevance of any security and quality requirements that are generated. The quality goals of the project must be in clear support of the project's overall business goal, which also must be identified and enumerated in this step.

Once the goals of the various stakeholders are identified, they must be reviewed, prioritized, and documented. In the absence of consensus, an executive decision may be needed to prioritize the goals.

The exit criteria for this step is to document a single *business goal* for the project and several prioritized *security and quality goals* for the overall software system.

2.1.3   Perform Risk Assessments

This step begins with identification of the vulnerabilities and threats that face the system, the likelihood that the threats will materialize as real attacks, and any potential consequences of an attack. Without a risk assessment, organizations may be tempted to implement security requirements or countermeasures without any logical rationale.

Once the threats have been identified by the risk assessment method, they must be classified according to their likelihood. These will aid in prioritizing the security requirements generated at a later stage. For each threat identified, a corresponding security requirement can identify a quantifiable and verifiable response. For instance, a requirement may describe speed of containment, cost of recovery, or limit to the damage that can be done to the system's functionality.

The requirements engineering team should facilitate the completion of a structured risk assessment, which is often performed by an external risk expert. Once complete, review the results of the risk assessment and share them with stakeholders.

The exit criteria for this step are documented threats, their likelihoods, and their classifications.

2.1.4   Elicit Security Requirements

Prior to this step, the requirements engineering team must select an elicitation technique that is suitable for the client organization and project. Multiple techniques may work for the same project. The difficulty with selecting a technique is choosing one that can adapt to the number and expertise of the stakeholders, the size and scope of the client project, and the expertise of the requirements engineering team.

CMU has done an extensive evaluation and analysis of the different types of elicitation methods and has shown that the Accelerated Requirements Method (ARM) has been successful for eliciting security requirements. The evaluation criteria include:

- *Adaptability*: The method can be used to generate requirements in multiple environments. For example, the elicitation method works equally as well with a software product that is near completion as with a project in the planning stages.
- *Computer-aided software engineering (CASE) tool*: The method includes a CASE tool. (The Software Engineering Institute defines a CASE tool as "a computer-based product aimed at supporting one or more software engineering activities within a software development process.")
- *Stakeholder acceptance*: The stakeholders are likely to agree to the elicitation method in analyzing their requirements. For example, the method isn't too invasive in a business environment.
- *Easy implementation*: The elicitation method isn't overly complex and can be properly executed easily.
- *Graphical output*: The method produces readily understandable visual artifacts.

- *Quick implementation*: The requirements engineers and stakeholders can fully execute the elicitation method in a reasonable length of time.
- *Shallow learning curve*: The requirements engineers and stakeholders can fully comprehend the elicitation method within a reasonable length of time.
- *High maturity*: The elicitation method has experienced considerable exposure and analysis in the requirements engineering community.
- *Scalability*: The method can be used to elicit the requirements of projects of different sizes, from enterprise-level systems to small-scale applications.[3]

Though results will vary from one organization to another, CMU's approach is worth considering as a choice for your organization.

The Security Elicitation step is the heart of the SQUARE process. This step describes the execution of the elicitation technique that was previously selected.

Avoiding Potential Mistakes

The biggest mistake that the requirements engineering team can make in this step is to elicit nonverifiable, vague, or ambiguous requirements. Each requirement must be stated in a manner that will enable relatively easy verification once the project has been implemented. For instance, the requirement "the system shall improve the availability of the existing customer service center" is impossible to measure objectively. Instead, the requirements engineering team should encourage the production of requirements that are clearly verifiable and, where appropriate, quantifiable. A better version of the previously stated requirement would thus be "The system shall handle at least 300 simultaneous connections to the customer service center." Later in this chapter, you'll learn what makes for a good write-up of nonfunctional requirements, and throughout the book you'll see hundreds of good examples.

A second mistake that the requirements engineering team can make in this step is to elicit *implementations* or *architectural constraints* instead of requirements. Requirements are concerned with *what* the system should do, not *how* it should be done.

Face-to-Face Elicitation Works Best

A key success factor is face-to-face interaction with all stakeholders. The exit Criteria is an *initial* set of documented nonfunctional requirements for the system.

Different methodologies dictate differing documentation techniques for requirements gathering and analysis. Fans of the Unified Modeling Language and Rational Unified Process are very familiar with the documentation tool called *use cases* to capture functional requirements, but you may find that they are not well-suited for capturing NFRs. You might find that *misuse cases* to describe the steps of performing a malicious act against a system are useful, just as you might describe an act that the system is supposed to perform in a use case. Here are some suggested steps to follow:

1.   Begin with a preexisting knowledge base of common security problems for systems that are similar to the one under development, and determine whether an attacker may have cause to think such vulnerability is possible in the system being developed. Then, try to describe how the attacker would leverage the problem. if it exists.

2.   Brainstorm on the basis of a list of system resources. For each resource, attempt to construct misuse cases in connection with each of the basic security services: authentication, confidentiality, access control, integrity, and availability.

3.   Third, brainstorm on the basis of a set of existing use cases. This may be useful for identifying representative risks and for ensuring that the first two approaches did not overlook any obvious threats. Misuse cases derived in this fashion are often written in terms of a valid use and then annotated to have malicious steps.[4]

2.1.5   Prioritize Requirements

In most cases, the development team will be unable to implement all of the nonfunctional requirements due to the lack of time and/or resources, or due to changes in the goals of the project. The purpose, then, of this step in the SQUARE process is to prioritize the nonfunctional requirements, so that the stakeholders can choose which requirements to implement and in which order.

During prioritization, some of the requirements may be deemed entirely infeasible to implement. In such cases, the requirements engineering team has a choice; completely dismiss the requirement from further consideration, or document the requirement as "future work" and remove it from the draft set of project requirements. This decision should be made after consulting with all the stakeholders and after leadership approvals.

2.2   Characteristics of Good Requirements

As you're collecting and documenting NFRs to include in analysis and design documentation, it's not important that every category of NFR has at least one or more specific requirement—requirements are not generally organized by which NFRs they meet. What is important is that your analysis is thorough and that all aspects of software quality are considered. What's also important is that these requirements be documented to meet the criteria of a "good" requirement statement. Table 2.1 lists some of the attributes for good requirements and may be used to help refine them as you document them.

Table 2.1   Characteristics of Good Requirements

Characteristic	Explanation
Cohesive	The requirement addresses one and only one thing.
Complete	The requirement is fully stated in one place with no missing information.
Consistent	The requirement does not contradict any other requirement and is fully consistent with all authoritative external documentation.
Correct	The requirement meets all or part of a business or resilience need as authoritatively stated by stakeholders.
Current	The requirement has not been made obsolete by the passage of time.
Externally Observable	The requirement specifies a characteristic of the product that is externally observable or experienced by the user.
Feasible	The requirement can be implemented within the constraints of the project.

Table 2.1 Characteristics of Good Requirements (continued)

Characteristic	Explanation
Unambiguous	The requirement is stated concisely, without unnecessary technical jargon, acronyms, or other esoteric terms or concepts. The requirement statement expresses objective fact, not subjective opinion. It is subject to one and only one interpretation. Vague subjects, adjectives, prepositions, verbs, and subjective phrases are avoided. Negative statements and compound statements are not used.
Mandatory	The requirement represents a stakeholder-defined characteristic or constraint.
Verifiable	Implementation of the requirement can be determined through one of four possible methods: inspection, analysis, demonstration, or test. If testing is the method needed for verifiability, the documentation should contain a section on how a tester might go about testing for it and what results would be considered passing.

Source: Wapedia Wiki: Requirements, http://wapedia.mobi/en/Requirements.

Another approach to ensuring that NFRs meet the characteristics of goodness uses the SMART mnemonic for their development:

- *Specific*—Is it without ambiguity, using consistent terminology, simple, and at the appropriate level of detail?
- *Measurable*—Can you verify that this requirement has been met? What tests must be performed, or what criteria must be met, to verify that the requirement is met?
- *Attainable*—Is it technically feasible? What is your professional judgment of the technical "do-ability" of the requirement?
- *Realistic*—Do you have the right resources? Is the right staff available? Do they have the right skills? Do you have enough time?
- *Traceable*—Is it linked from its conception through its specification to its subsequent design, implementation, and test?[5]

2.3 Summary

There's no question that deriving nonfunctional requirements in software development projects can be a daunting and enormous task that requires dozens of labor-hours from a cross-section of people who have a stake in the road, where maintenance, support, and operational costs quickly negate any benefits the software was planned to provide.

In Chapter 2 you learned about CMU's SQUARE methodology for deriving NFR and what constitutes well-developed and well-written NFRs.

In Chapter 3, we'll begin to peel the onion, first looking at resilience and software quality categories of NFRs and cover requirements related to the application software and the operating environment. Chapter 4 then digs into security NFRs for applications and Chapter 5 into security infrastructure services for the operating environment.

2.4 Notes

1. John Mylopoulos, Lawrence Chung, Brian A. Nixon, and Eric Yu. *Non-functional requirements in software engineering*, University of Texas Dallas. accessed February 22,2011, www.utdallas.edu/~chung/BOOK/book.html.

2. "SQUARE Instructional Materials," Software Engineering Institute, accessed February 22, 2011, www.cert.org/sse/square/square-description.html.

3. "Requirements Elicitation Case Studies Using IBIS, JAD, and ARM," *Build Security In*, accessed February 23, 2011, https://buildsecurityin.us-cert.gov/bsi/articles/best-practices/requirements/532-BSI.html.

4. "Detail Misuse Cases," OWASP.org, accessed February 27, 2011, www.owasp.org/index.php/Detail_misuse_cases.

5. "Architecture Resources for Enterprise Advantage." Breedmeyer Consulting Web site, accessed February 27, 2011, www.ewita.com/newsletters/10023Files/NonFunctReq.PDF.

Chapter 3

Resilience and Quality for Applications and Runtime Environments

The features that characterize software as *resilient* cover lots of ground. While implementing appropriate security controls helps with software's ability to "bounce back" from disruptive events, there are a host of other necessary features for a resilient application. Some of these features and controls require effort at the application itself, while others require effort for the infrastructures under which applications run. Some are required for both, enabling an application to take advantage of infrastructure security or other services.

In Chapter 3, we'll dig into the details of nonfunctional requirements related to the "ilities" or quality aspects of application software and software operations: scalability, extensibility, portability, serviceability, and others.

Most of the features or characteristics you'll find here are intended to further refine the functional requirements you develop for customized software. In other words, as you're thinking about *what the software must do*, you should also be thinking about *how well the software must do it*. These requirements are meant to constrain the functional requirements or provide quality controls and resilience into the functions. Since these features are specific to functions and how well you need them to work, you'll need to document these qualities and characteristics directly in the requirement descriptions for each function.

3.1 Relationships among Nonfunctional Requirements

The ISO/IEC 9126-1 Standard is a useful model[1] for understanding software quality and its attributes in context. This standard focuses software quality requirements through a system perspective and shows the hierarchy of quality aspects of software, as illustrated in Figure 3.1.

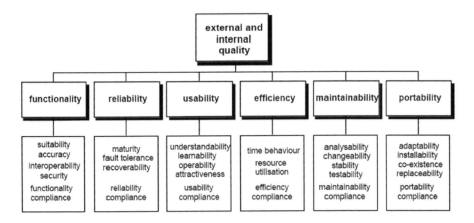

Figure 3.1 Relationships among Nonfunctional Requirements

It's not important that you describe quality requirements in every category, but it is important to consider your needs for quality in every function and every process that you document as required for the software you intend to develop.

3.2 Considerations for Developing NFRs for your Applications and Runtime Environment

Table 3.1 lists the software quality attributes from ISO/IEC 9126-1 along with subcharacteristics and definitions to help you to determine which characteristics you'll need for new or modified application software.

Table 3.1 ISO/IEC 9126-1 Software Quality Attributes

Attribute	Subcharacteristic	Definition
Functionality	Suitability	Attributes of software that bear on the presence and appropriateness of a set of functions for specified tasks
	Accurateness	Attributes of software that bear on the provision of right or agreed-upon results or effects
	Interoperability	Attributes of software that bear on its ability to interact with specified systems

Table 3.1   ISO/IEC 9126-1 Software Quality Attributes (continued)

Attribute	Subcharacteristic	Definition
	Compliance	Attributes of software that make the software adhere to application-related standards, conventions, or regulations in laws and similar prescriptions
	Security	Attributes of software that bear on its ability to prevent unauthorized access, whether accidental or deliberate, to programs or data
Reliability	Maturity	Attributes of software that bear on the frequency of failure by faults in the software
	Fault tolerance	Attributes of software that bear on its ability to maintain a specified level of performance in case of software faults or of infringement of its specified interface
	Recoverability	Attributes of software that bear on the capability to reestablish its level of performance and recover the data directly affected in case of a failure, and on the time and effort needed to do so
Usability	Understandability	Attributes of software that bear on the users' effort necessary to recognize the logical concept and its applicability
	Learnability	Attributes of software that bear on the users' effort necessary to learn its application
	Operability	Attributes of software that bear on the users' effort necessary for operation and operation control

Table 3.1   ISO/IEC 9126-1 Software Quality Attributes (continued)

Attribute	Subcharacteristic	Definition
Efficiency	Time behavior	Attributes of software that bear on response and processing times and on throughput rates in performing its function
	Resource behavior	Attributes of software that bear on the amount of resources used and the duration of such use in performing its function
Maintainability	Analyzability	Attributes of software that bear on the effort needed for diagnosis of deficiencies or causes of failures, or for identification of parts to be modified
	Changeability	Attributes of software that bear on the effort needed for modification, fault removal, or environmental change
	Stability	Attributes of software that bear on the risk of unexpected effect of modifications
	Testability	Attributes of software that bear on the effort needed for validating the modified software
Portability	Adaptability	Attributes of software that bear on the opportunity for the software to be adapted to different specified environments, without applying actions or means other than those provided for this purpose for the software considered
	Install-ability	Attributes of software that bear on the effort needed to install the software in a specified environment

Table 3.1   ISO/IEC 9126-1 Software Quality Attributes (continued)

Attribute	Subcharacteristic	Definition
	Conformance	Attributes of software that make the software adhere to standards or conventions relating to portability
	Replaceability	Attributes of software that bear on opportunity and effort necessary for using it in the place of specified other software in the environment of that software

Source: ISO 9126 Software Quality Standards

Driving down into further detail in each category, Table 3.2 offers a comprehensive laundry list of NFRs for resilience and quality. To further help you come up with the right questions, you'll find a set of considerations for defining quality requirements, followed by a checklist to make sure that you've covered all the bases.

As you'll see, security shows up in virtually every category, but you'll find the specific application security and privacy requirements documented in Chapter 4.

Table 3.2, adapted from an EDS worksheet[2] for use on client projects, is intended to serve as a checklist of nonfunctional requirements to be considered by requirements analysts for creating a correct and complete requirements document. Not all of the NFR categories will apply to all projects. Subject matter experts from around the organizations will be needed to help make these relevant and practical for each specific project. These sources should include:

- Technical architects
- Chief technologists
- Network specialists
- Security specialists
- Training specialists
- Legal specialists
- Financial specialists
- Documentation specialists
- Data center specialists

- Operations support specialists
- Auditors
- Database administrators

Table 3.2   Considerations for Developing NFRs

Nonfunctional Requirement Category	Description and Considerations
Auditability	These requirements address the need for the application to be auditable. Considerations include: ■ Who will perform the audits ■ Standards to be applied ■ Frequency of the audits ■ How noncompliance issues will be handled ■ Fault and failure recording and tracking These requirements address the need to trace or log use of the system. Considerations include: ■ Who visited a Web page ■ Who read or updated a database ■ Who read or updated a program ■ What operations were performed
Availability	These requirements define when the application is available. Considerations include: ■ System uptime ■ Defined maintenance window ■ Dependence on other systems ■ Restore and reactivate procedures ■ Alternative processes and fail-over plans ■ Cost of availability (cost per transaction, including support) ■ Cost of unavailability (cost of impact to organization)

Table 3.2   Considerations for Developing NFRs (continued)

Nonfunctional Requirement Category	Description and Considerations
Backup and Restore	These requirements address plans and provisions for backup and restore operations. Considerations include: ■ Named items for backup operations (data, programs) ■ Responsibilities for performing backup and restore operations ■ Storage medium ■ Volume ■ Storage location (on and off site) ■ Frequency and timing of backup operations ■ Data retention ■ Hot backups ■ Transportation to storage facilities ■ Facilities ■ Handling ■ Cataloging ■ Security ■ Retrieval ■ Procedures to request restoration
Capacity Planning	These requirements address the system load at any given time. Considerations include: ■ Memory ■ Database size ■ Throughput ■ Number of users ■ Number of transactions processed ■ Rate of growth

Table 3.2   Considerations for Developing NFRs (continued)

Nonfunctional Requirement Category	Description and Considerations
Conversion	These requirements address the need for the application or application components to undergo onetime or ongoing transition activities. Considerations include: ■ Ongoing file format conversion for interface with another application ■ One-time file format conversion for data loads ■ Data migration ■ Special data validation and conversion software ■ Automated conversion tools ■ Periodic upgrades of hardware and software ■ One-time transition of an application to a new application or platform ■ One-time transition of computer resources to a new product line ■ Training in the old and new environments to support conversion ■ Training in the new environment for ongoing support ■ Temporary acquisition of subject matter experts to support conversion ■ Phased conversion ■ Parallel operations for testing and training

Table 3.2   Considerations for Developing NFRs (continued)

Nonfunctional Requirement Category	Description and Considerations
Data Integrity	These requirements address the integrity of data. Considerations include: ■ Timeliness (how current must information be) ■ Database replication ■ Process sequencing ■ Language translation ■ Accuracy (specific values, free text) ■ Data quality ■ Referential integrity ■ Content ■ Format ■ Robustness
Data Retention	These requirements address the need to retain data after it is no longer considered active. Considerations include: ■ Archiving procedures ■ Backup and restore operations ■ Purges ■ Shelf life ■ Storage medium ■ Volume

Table 3.2   Considerations for Developing NFRs (continued)

Nonfunctional Requirement Category	Description and Considerations
Development Environment	These requirements address special arrangements made in the development environment in support of the project. Considerations include: ■ Hardware ■ Software ■ Licenses ■ Responsibilities for research, purchase, and ownership of hardware, software, and licenses ■ Developer training ■ Relocation ■ Facilities ■ Additional phone lines ■ Security ■ Servers ■ Network ■ Databases ■ Memory ■ Compilers ■ Testing tools ■ Test data source ■ Special testing requirements

Table 3.2   Considerations for Developing NFRs (continued)

Nonfunctional Requirement Category	Description and Considerations
Documentation	These requirements address specific documentation provided as a project deliverable. Considerations include: ▪ Target audience or recipient ▪ Architecture diagrams ▪ Technical manuals ▪ User instructions (format and content) ▪ Online help facilities ▪ Multilingual capabilities ▪ System overview documents ▪ Data models ▪ Code ▪ Organization's documentation standards and templates
Economics	These requirements address economic specifications for the project. Considerations include: ▪ Minimum profit increase ▪ Minimum cost reduction ▪ Budgetary limits on development or operating costs ▪ Maximum cost per transaction ▪ Maximum cost per user
Efficiency	These requirements address application efficiency, in the sense that there are no wasted or duplicated efforts and minimal planned delays. Considerations include: ▪ Anticipated user error rate ▪ Speed and accuracy of processing ▪ Process flow ▪ Duplicated effort or tasks with other processes or systems ▪ Interaction with nonautomated processes and activities ▪ Business process reengineering

Table 3.2   Considerations for Developing NFRs (continued)

Nonfunctional Requirement Category	Description and Considerations
Hardware	These requirements address specific hardware considerations for a project. Considerations include: ■ Named vendors or applications ■ Existing vendor contracts ■ Existing purchase agreements ■ Existing hardware ■ Hardware/software compatibility ■ Infrastructure and installation compatibility ■ Size parameters ■ Organization's technical direction
Infrastructure	These requirements address the infrastructure necessary for the development, operation, and support of the application. Considerations include: ■ Accessibility to facilities, equipment, or system ■ Utilities (electrical, water, climate control) ■ Electrical backup (generators) ■ Phone lines ■ Network services ■ Performance requirements ■ Support requirements ■ Physical environment ■ Existing infrastructure

Table 3.2   Considerations for Developing NFRs (continued)

Nonfunctional Requirement Category	Description and Considerations
Installability	These requirements address the ease with which the application is installed in the user's environment. Considerations include: ■ Responsibilities ■ Timing of installations ■ Locations ■ Number of installations ■ Dependencies in the installation schedule ■ Required infrastructure ■ Hardware/software version compatibilities ■ Installation guides (format, content, multilingual requirements) ■ Installation procedures (automated or manual) ■ Installation package (instructions, CD, downloads) ■ Procedures for installing patches and upgrades ■ Application release or upgrade schedule

Table 3.2   Considerations for Developing NFRs (continued)

Nonfunctional Requirement Category	Description and Considerations
International Use	These requirements address special issues associated with the developing, implementing, and supporting an application or system that is used internationally. Considerations include: ■ Customs regulations ■ Security ■ Transportation ■ Language translation ■ Special character fonts ■ Communication ■ Fees (taxes, duties, tariffs) ■ Local contractors ■ Responsibilities ■ Licensing ■ Encryption ■ Work permits ■ Passports and visas ■ Export compliance
Interoperability	These requirements address the need for the application to interface with other applications or systems without interfering with the operation of those other applications or systems. Considerations include: ■ Named applications or systems with which to interface ■ Messaging format, medium, and content ■ Compatibility with applications from different vendors ■ Conversion requirements for hardware, applications, or data ■ Middleware architecture ■ Messaging and transmission protocols ■ Frequency ■ Multiple time zones ■ Process timing and sequencing

Table 3.2   Considerations for Developing NFRs (continued)

Nonfunctional Require-ment Category	Description and Considerations
Legal	These requirements address legal constraints that are not covered in the functional requirements. Considerations include: ■ Laws ■ Government regulations and standards ■ Labor contracts ■ Uses and export/import of cryptography ■ Supplier contracts ■ Intellectual property protection ■ Copyrights ■ Patents ■ Export compliance

Table 3.2   Considerations for Developing NFRs (continued)

Nonfunctional Requirement Category	Description and Considerations
Maintainability	These requirements address the ease that the software accepts repairs or adapts to new functionality. Requirements are needed to address the processes where problems are reported and resolved. Considerations include: ■ Defined maintenance window ■ Maintenance across time zones ■ Procedure for emergency fixes ■ Mean time to repair ■ Support logistics (onsite, remote help desk) ■ Third-party service contracts ■ Process for problem reporting and escalation ■ Procedure for logging and tracking defects ■ Root cause analysis of defects ■ Application release or upgrade schedule ■ Change request process ■ Support responsibilities ■ Organization's business direction ■ Organization's technical direction ■ Standards that ensure the application is modifiable within budgeted time and resources ■ Procedures to change run-time control or schedule parameters ■ Routine diagnostic checks

Table 3.2   Considerations for Developing NFRs (continued)

Nonfunctional Requirement Category	Description and Considerations
Environment	These requirements address special considerations for the model office environment in support of the project. Considerations include: ■ Database ■ Memory ■ Data ■ Server ■ Network ■ Hardware ■ Software ■ Licenses ■ Responsibilities for research, purchase, and ownership of hardware, software and licenses ■ Software version compatibility ■ Security ■ Special testing requirements

Table 3.2   Considerations for Developing NFRs (continued)

Nonfunctional Requirement Category	Description and Considerations
Operating Environment	These requirements address special considerations for the operation and ongoing support of the delivered application. Considerations include: ■ Number of users ■ Database size ■ Memory ■ System availability ■ Event/job/process scheduling ■ System dependencies ■ Support and change request procedures ■ Problem escalation procedures ■ Roles and responsibilities ■ Hardware ■ Software ■ Licenses ■ Responsibilities for research, purchase, and ownership of hardware, software, and licenses ■ Support contracts (hardware, software) ■ Documentation ■ Monitoring procedures ■ Alarm or action triggers ■ Response to triggers ■ Training and certifications ■ Location ■ Security ■ Procedures to change runtime control or schedule parameters

Table 3.2   Considerations for Developing NFRs (continued)

Nonfunctional Requirement Category	Description and Considerations
Performance	These requirements address system performance. Considerations include: ■ Data throughput ■ Response time for transactions (real, perceived, expected) ■ System capacity ■ Speed and accuracy of processing ■ Network latency (local, national, and international usage) ■ Network routing options ■ Line speed ■ Load distribution based on activities, events, dates, transactions, or users ■ Load distribution over time (hourly, daily weekly, monthly, or yearly cycles) ■ Impact of geographic diversity ■ Average ■ Spikes ■ Peaks ■ Data volume ■ Server load ■ Multiple applications running simultaneously on shared components of the system (Web server, application server, database server) ■ Organization's business direction (including mergers, acquisitions, and expansions) ■ Organization's technical direction ■ Historic metrics ■ Complete system operation (security, servers, databases, and network)

Table 3.2   Considerations for Developing NFRs (continued)

Nonfunctional Requirement Category	Description and Considerations
Physical Environment	These requirements address the physical environment in which the application must function. Considerations include: ■ Location (indoors/outdoors, office/factory/warehouse) ■ Number of locations ■ Diversity of locations ■ Temperature and climate constraints ■ Dimension constraints ■ Weight constraints ■ Stability/mobility ■ Safety ■ Durability
Portability	These requirements address the ease with which the application is implemented on or migrated to other platforms or operating systems. Considerations include: ■ Named platforms on which the application must function ■ Platform-dependent languages or utilities ■ Ability to migrate to other platforms ■ n-tier architectures ■ Organization's technical direction ■ Organization's business direction ■ Existing platforms

Table 3.2   Considerations for Developing NFRs (continued)

Nonfunctional Require-ment Category	Description and Considerations
Procedures	These requirements address the processes, methods, procedures, or standards that will be followed in the development and support of the application. Considerations include: ■ Organization's policies ■ Industry standards ■ Certification to the organization's standards ■ Named tools ■ Templates ■ Coding standards ■ Testing standards ■ Documentation standards

Recoverability	These requirements address the ability to recover from unexpected interruptions, including:
	■ Power failures
	■ Application failures
	■ Lost data
	■ Sabotage
	■ Acts of nature
	■ Acts of war, terrorism, or vandalism
	■ Considerations include:
	  ◎ Acceptable response time to recover
	  ◎ Mission criticality of applications
	  ◎ Responsibilities
	  ◎ Organizational practices and standards
	  ◎ Disaster recovery drills
	  ◎ System backup and restore procedures
	  ◎ Data- and system-level recovery
	  ◎ Alternative practices and fail-over plans
	  ◎ Back-out procedures for a midtransaction crash
	  ◎ Penalties for failure to recover in acceptable times

Table 3.2   Considerations for Developing NFRs (continued)

Nonfunctional Requirement Category	Description and Considerations
Redundancy	These requirements address the ability to replace a failed component with another component, i.e. the degree of availability, or fault-tolerance, of the system or infrastructure. Considerations include: ■ Duplicate components ■ Automatic fail-over ■ Transaction level integrity ■ Replicated database
Reliability	These requirements address the acceptable defect rate or failure rate of the delivered application. Considerations include: ■ Degree to which the application performs to expectations ■ Anticipated frequency or timing of failures ■ Expected cause of failures ■ Acceptable recovery time (downtime) ■ Mechanism for recording and tracking faults and failures
Reproducibility	These requirements address the ability of the application to be re-created or replicated. Considerations include: ■ Actions to make illegal reproduction difficult ■ Procedures to reproduce a application for replacement ■ Procedures for installation at additional user sites

Table 3.2   Considerations for Developing NFRs (continued)

Nonfunctional Requirement Category	Description and Considerations
Resource Management	These requirements address responsibilities for acquisition or monitoring of personnel and equipment for the development, operation, and support of the application. Considerations include: ■ Lead time on equipment orders and installation ■ Training requirements ■ Specification of special skills ■ Ordering, installation, and maintenance, of equipment ■ Budget constraints ■ Supplier contracts
Responsibilities	These requirements address the need to associate people to the tasks for which they are responsible: ■ Individual people ■ Roles ■ Teams ■ Groups ■ Job functions ■ Organizations/departments ■ Government agencies ■ Suppliers ■ Subcontractors
Reusability	These requirements address the ease with which the application or a application component is reused, or converted for use, in the same project or another project.

Table 3.2   Considerations for Developing NFRs (continued)

Nonfunctional Requirement Category	Description and Considerations
Robustness	These requirements address how the application will respond to: ■ Data exceptions ■ System failures ■ Hardware failures Considerations include: ■ Alarms and triggers ■ System response ■ Levels of severity ■ Organization policies and processes for such events ■ Fault and failure recording and tracking
Scalability	These requirements address the ability of the application to adapt to new technologies and to changes in postimplementation metrics. Considerations include: ■ Ability of the application to accommodate application upgrades and new functionality (application releases) ■ Change in throughput ■ Change in the number of users ■ Change in the number of transactions processed ■ Change in level of support ■ Change in memory requirements ■ Horizontal scalability (adding similar components) ■ Vertical scalability (adding capacity to existing components) ■ Organization's business direction (including mergers, acquisitions, expansions, and divestitures) ■ Organization's technical direction

Table 3.2 Considerations for Developing NFRs (continued)

Nonfunctional Requirement Category	Description and Considerations
Training	These requirements address commitments for training the organization's users as a result of the project. These requirements address training to be provided to the project team in support of project activities. Considerations include: ▪ Training provider ▪ Types of training (end user, technical, vendor) ▪ Cost ▪ Budget allowance ▪ Financial arrangements ▪ Facilities ▪ Location ▪ Timing ▪ Forum ▪ Materials ▪ Frequency ▪ Duration ▪ Preparation ▪ Prerequisites ▪ Participants ▪ Security ▪ Training environment for the system (database, server, network, application, data) ▪ Ongoing support for training materials, plans, and the training environment

Table 3.2   Considerations for Developing NFRs (continued)

Nonfunctional Requirement Category	Description and Considerations
Usability	These requirements address the ease with which a person uses the application. Considerations include: ■ Productivity level of the end user (anticipated error rate) ■ User's experience level (novice or highly trained) ■ Diversity in user skills ■ Minimum/maximum level of training or support required ■ Frequency of application use ■ Compatibility or consistency with other organization's applications ■ Aesthetics (volume, brightness, color schemes) ■ Type of user interaction (real-time, one-way, visual, audible) ■ System response to errors and invalid data entry ■ Assistance (online help, remote help, problem escalation) ■ Degree of user interaction (close monitoring, periodic inspection) ■ Multilingual capabilities (for displays, manuals, online help, fonts, translation) ■ Navigation ■ Instructions (format, content) ■ Physical limitations of the user ■ Interoperability with existing workflows and user processes

Source: adapted from "Non-functional Requirements Checklist," Fish, Gilbert & Associates, LLC.

3.3   Checking Your Work

The following checklist shown in Table 3.3, adapted from *Observations from a Tech Architect: Enterprise Implementation Issues & Solutions*[3], provides a high-level view of quality requirements to help you determine whether quality and resilience are adequately addressed as you're in the last stages of developing systems analysis documentation.

By addressing these higher-level questions, you can gain assurance that all the right questions related to software quality have been asked of the right people at the right times.

Table 3.3   Requirements Gathering Phase Completion Checklist

	YES	NO	N/A	Remarks
Has the customer established the important quality considerations from the users' perspective that will determine whether the application meets user requirements?				
Has the project team worked with the acceptor to define a maximum of 10 quality factors ranked in order of importance, the top three (+/-) being the customer's critical success factors?				
Does the acceptor understand and agree to any tradeoffs that must be made between conflicting factors (e.g., maintainability versus efficiency)?				
Has each quality factor been translated into one or more application-related quality criteria that can be used to measure the attainment of each quality factor (e.g., modularity is an example of a quality criteria that could be used to measure maintainability)?				
Have metrics been defined to measure each of the quality criteria?				

Table 3.3 Requirements Gathering Phase Completion Checklist (continued)

	YES	NO	N/A	Remarks
Have data collection and analysis methods been defined for each quality metric, including the data collection frequency?				
Have thresholds or targets and specific improvement goals been defined for each quality metric?				

Source: adapted from *Observations from a Tech Architect: Enterprise Implementation Issues & Solutions.*

3.4 Summary

Deriving nonfunctional requirements for software development projects is a daunting task that takes dozens of person-hours from a wide cross-section of people across the enterprise. Regardless of the efforts needed up front, ignoring NFRs or making a conscious decision to eliminate them from software designs only kicks the problem down the road, where increased maintenance, support, and operational costs quickly reverse any of the benefits the software was planned to provide. Costs to address these issues can increase later by one hundredfold[4].

Chapter 3 is designed to help you to create a comprehensive requirements document that answers most questions that will come up in later phases of development.

In Chapter 4, we'll peel the onion further to reveal 93 explicit security functional requirements for your applications. Chapter 5 examines how to implement security as a service to your applications by imbedding it into your operating infrastructure.

3.5 Notes

1. ISO/IEC 9126-1, 2001, *Information Technology—Software Engineering Product Quality, Part 1: Quality Model*, accessed April 21, 2011, www.iso.org/iso/iso_catalogue/catalogue_tc/catalogue_detail.htm?csnumber=22749

2.   "Non-Functional Requirements Checklist," Fish, Gilbert & Associates, LLC, accessed April 21, 2011, www.hfgilbert.com/rc/CBAP/Ch3/Non-functional_Requirements_Checklist.pdf.

3.   "Defining Quality Requirements Checklist," Toolbox for IT. accessed May 12, 2011, http://it.toolbox.com/blogs/enterprise-solutions/defining-quality-requirements-checklist-26106.

4.   Barry W. Boehm and Richard Turner, *Balancing Agility and Discipline: a Guide for the Perplexed* (Boston, MA: Addison-Wesley, 2006).

Chapter 4

Security Requirements for Application Software

Information security requirements for any software development efforts derive from two key sources:

- *Generic*: Best practices and attack patterns
- *Application-specific*: Abuse case and risk analysis

Chapter 4 provides a comprehensive set of reusable security requirements that were developed or derived from industry best practices and historical application software risks and vulnerabilities. These requirements are usable directly or, like the earlier sets of NFRs you saw, will serve as food for thought and can be adapted to fit your specific applications. Each requirement addresses one aspect of security controls implementation. To better understand how a requirement dictates a control objective, it's important to understand the different types of information security controls.

4.1 Security Control Types

Security controls fall into two categories.

The first category describes what the control *actually is*: an administrative, technical, or physical control–for example,a named process, a standard, a firewall, a locked door, or the like.

- *Administrative controls* are generally the policies, standards, and procedures that guide employees when conducting the organization's business.
- *Technical controls* are the devices, protocols, and other technology used to protect assets. These could include antivirus systems, cryptographic systems, firewalls, etc.
- *Physical controls* are controls that have to do with the physical facility: locked doors and the like.

The second category describes what the control *does*: prevent, detect, and correct (response or recovery).

- *Preventative security controls* are needed to prevent intentional or unintentional security threats.
- *Detective or response controls* act like alarms and warnings. These controls kick in after an incident begins. Examples include motion detectors, log files, files that contain system audit information, and the like.
- *Corrective controls* are needed for responding to and fixing a security incident. Corrective controls are also used to limit or stop further damage. Some examples might include closing off a firewall port, blocking an IP address, and so on.
- *Recovery controls* are needed to help put a system back into operation once the incident ends.

There is often overlap between controls–some can be administrative and preventative, or technical and corrective, or any combination you can think of. This overlap occurs on purpose as an implementation of the principle of Defense in Depth.

4.2   Think Like an Attacker

As you begin working with these 93 requirements, you might consider some of them as odd or unusual. Typical application development teams are usually too focused on making an application do *what they want it to do*, rather than considering *what the application should NOT do* or considering ways that malicious or curious people attack software applications. Our goal here then is to help you consider an attacker's mindset by taking into account what makes an application fail or collapse when attacked and then provide you with the requirements to prevent those failures and eliminate the vulnerabilities that may be exploited.

While we *do not* advocate that business application developers write the security functions that implement many of these requirements, we do recommend that they be included in all system specifications to ensure that developers are taking advantage of security frameworks like OWASP's Enterprise Security APIs, and for testers to ensure that the requirements are present and are implemented correctly. Writing security functions is very different from using them, but the need for documenting required functions is vital to the overall security and resilience of applications.

4.3   Detailed Security Requirements

The following pages of security requirements were drawn or developed using the Common Criteria for Information Technology Security Evaluation, Part 2: Security Functional Components,[1] The AICPA's Generally Accepted Privacy Principles[2] and The BITS Master Security Criteria.[3] These requirements are organized and listed using the following security topic classifications:

- Identification requirements
- Authentication requirements
- Authorization requirements
- Security auditing requirements
- Confidentiality requirements
- Integrity requirements
- Availability requirements
- Non-repudiation requirements
- Immunity requirements
- Survivability requirements
- Systems maintenance security requirements
- Privacy requirements

Sometimes these requirements blur the lines between categories. You can use the tags/subcategories for better clarity or specificity.

4.4   Identification Requirements

Identification requirements specify the extent to which a business, application, or component, *identifies* external entities (e.g., humans, external applications, etc.) before interacting with them.[4]

Table 4.1 documents the requirement for Unique User IDs.

Table 4.1   Unique User ID Requirements

Req. ID: SR-IDEN-001	Category: SECURITY
Subcategory(ies)/Tags	Identification, User ID, Login
Name	Unique User ID
Requirement	The software system shall uniquely identified each user of the system with a unique user ID

Table 4.1   Unique User ID Requirements (continued)

Use Case(s)	Initial login to the system
Rationale	It is of utmost importance to identify individual users to provide reliable accountability for actions. Shared accounts prevent accountability and auditability of actions performed on a system.
Priority	**Critical**/High/Medium/Low
Constraints	NA
Comments	A user may be a human, an automated process or another system that requests a session with the system under consideration to perform a task. A user may have multiple user IDs as long as the multiple user IDs unambiguously and uniquely identify the user.
Test Case Ref #	STC-IDEN-001

Table 4.2 describes the requirement for preventing back doors in authentication systems.

Table 4.2   Preventing Back Doors in Authentication Systems

Req. ID: SR-IDEN-002	Category: SECURITY
Subcategory(ies)/Tags	Identification, User ID, Login, Backdoor
Name	Backdoor Prevention
Requirement	All interfaces of the software that are accessed for performing any action shall have the capability to recognize the user ID.
Use Case(s)	Initial login to the system, batch jobs, API calls, N/W interface
Rationale	Identification must be applied across all system interfaces. In the event that a "backdoor" exists through which access is granted with no identification, the security of the system would be compromised.
Priority	Critical/**High**/Medium/Low
Constraints	NA

Table 4.2   Preventing Back Doors in Authentication Systems (continued)

Comments	The term "interface" refers to the point of entry into a system. It can be a network interface, user interface, or other system interface, as appropriate.
Test Case Ref #	STC-IDEN-002-1, STC-IDEN-002-2

Table 4.3 describes the requirement for a process identifier code to establish accountability.

Table 4.3   Process Identifier Code Requirements

Req. ID: SR-IDEN-003	Category: SECURITY
Subcategory(ies)/Tags	Identification, User ID, Login, PID
Name	Process Identifier Code/Accountability
Requirement	For each process running in the system that has been initiated by a user, the system shall associate the process with the user ID of that specific user. Autonomous processes (such as a print spooler) shall be associated with an identifier code, such as "system ownership."
Use Case(s)	Process Spawning, Batch Jobs, etc.
Rationale	For identification to properly provide accountability, specific actions must be tied to the initiator of that action. This includes long-term and short-term processes running on the system.
Priority	Critical/**High**/Medium/Low
Constraints	NA
Comments	NA
Test Case Ref #	STC-IDEN-003

Table 4.4 describes the requirement for autodisabling user IDs.

Table 4.4   Autodisable User IDs

Req. ID: SR-IDEN-004	Category: SECURITY
Subcategory(ies)/Tags	Identification, User ID, Credentials
Name	Autodisable User IDs
Requirement	The application shall have the capability to automatically disable an identifier if it remains inactive for a specified time period (e.g., 90 days).
Use Case(s)	Auto expiration of temp user IDs
Rationale	Accounts that remain active, but dormant or unused, are often the targets of attack. The disabling process need not be automatic. For example, the system may generate an autonomous message for the administrator indicating that a user ID has remained inactive for the specified period. It is expected that the administrator will disable the user ID. However, an automatic disabling feature shall exist that the administrator may enable.
Priority	Critical/High/**Medium**/Low
Constraints	NA
Comments	Process level controls for routinely auditing and disabling unused user IDs shall exist.
Test Case Ref #	STC-IDEN-004

Table 4.5 describes the requirement for maintaining security attributes.

Table 4.5   Security Attributes

Req. ID: SR-IDEN-005	Category: SECURITY
Subcategory(ies)/Tags	Identification, User ID, Security Metadata
Name	Security Attributes

Table 4.5 Security Attributes (continued)

Requirement	The application/system shall maintain the following list of security attributes for each user: user ID, group memberships, access control privileges, authentication information, and security-relevant roles.
Use Case(s)	Autoexpiration of temp user IDs
Rationale	
Priority	Critical/High/**Medium**/Low
Constraints	NA
Comments	NA
Test Case Ref #	STC-IDEN-005

4.5 Authentication Requirements

An authentication requirement is any security requirement that specifies the extent to which a business, application, component, or center shall verify the identity of its externals (e.g., human actors and external applications) before interacting with them.[4]

Table 4.6 describes the requirement for credential security.

Table 4.6 Credential Security

Req. ID: SR-ATEN-001	Category: SECURITY
Subcategory(ies)/Tags	Authentication, Credentials, Passwords, Hashing
Name	Credential Security
Requirement	The system shall store the information used for authentication in a secure manner, using public and widely accepted cryptoalgorithms.
Use Case(s)	Password Storage
Rationale	Authenticating information must be stored in such a way so that a third party without authorization to do so cannot easily obtain it. For example, static passwords should be passed through a one-hash function, and only the hash should be stored.

Table 4.6   Credential Security (continued)

Priority	**Critical**/High/Medium/Low
Constraints	NA
Comments	Per-user salting is recommended for storing password hashing to provide additional level of security.
Test Case Ref #	STC-ATEN-001

Table 4.7 describes the requirement for replay attack protection.

Table 4.7   Replay Attack Protection

Req. ID: SR-ATEN-002	Category: SECURITY
Subcategory(ies)/Tags	Authentication, Credentials, Login, Replay Attack
Name	Replay Attack Protection
Requirement	The authentication process of the application shall protect the system from replay attacks by not only protecting the transmitted authentication information but also examining sequences of submitted authentication information.
Use Case(s)	Biometric-Based Login
Rationale	If transmissions of credentials can be eavesdropped upon, then it may be possible to replay the authenticator and convince the relying party that this is a new authentication attempt.
Priority	**Critical**/High/Medium/Low
Constraints	NA
Comments	This requirement is applicable for time-bound passwords and biometric authentication credentials and not for regular passwords.
Test Case Ref #	STC-ATEN-002

Table 4.8 describes the requirement for protecting against credential guessing to counter brute-force attacks on password systems.

Table 4.8   Protect Credential Guessing

Req. ID: SR-ATEN-003	Category: SECURITY
Subcategory(ies)/Tags	Authentication, Credential Enumeration, Login
Name	Protect Credential Guessing
Requirement	The system shall not provide feedback to the user during the authentication procedure other than "invalid" (i.e., it shall not reveal which part of the authentication [e.g., user ID or password] procedure is incorrect).
Use Case(s)	User Login
Rationale	Feedback that is too descriptive can inadvertently give out information regarding which part of an authentication procedure is incorrect, thus allowing an attacker to narrow his or her search.
Priority	Critical/**High**/Medium/Low
Constraints	Some other application flows (user registration/signup) may actually give up this information indirectly.
Comments	As long as strong brute-force detection and protection exists, the application shall be able to maintain good security levels against this type of attack.
Test Case Ref #	STC-ATEN-003

Table 4.9 describes the requirement for authenticating the server.

Table 4.9   Server Authentication

Req. ID: SR-ATEN-004	Category: SECURITY
Subcategory(ies)/Tags	Authentication, Credentials, Login
Name	Server Authentication
Requirement	The system shall have the ability to authenticate itself to the user and to other systems during session establishment.

Table 4.9   Server Authentication (continued)

Use Case(s)	Login over SSL into a Web application
Rationale	In most cases, authentication focuses solely on the client authentication to the server. However, without proper server-to-client authentication, it may be possible for a third party to impersonate a server and obtain client's authentication credentials.
Priority	**Critical**/High/Medium/Low
Constraints	With mechanisms such as SSH, Time of First Use (TOFU) problems exist.
Comments	Other authentication mechanisms where this requirement is not met shall be disabled or redirected to this form authentication (e.g., http to https).
Test Case Ref #	STC-ATEN-004

Table 4.10 describes the requirement for reauthentication.

Table 4.10   Reauthentication

Req. ID: SR-ATEN-005	Category: SECURITY
Subcategory(ies)/Tags	Authentication, Credentials, Login
Name	Reauthentication
Requirement	The system shall have the ability to reauthenticate the user during an active session.
Use Case(s)	Before performing critical transactions
Rationale	Periodic reauthentication improves a system's ability to withstand session "hijacking" attacks, in which a third party assumes control of a previously authenticated session.
Priority	Critical/**High**/Medium/Low
Constraints	NA

Table 4.10   Reauthentication (continued)

Comments	Other risk management and fraud detection/prevention controls shall exist for the primary protection of the application data.
Test Case Ref #	STC-ATEN-005

Table 4.11 describes the requirement for protecting credentials.

Table 4.11   Protection of Credentials

Req. ID: SR-ATEN-006	Category: SECURITY
Subcategory(ies)/Tags	Authentication, Credentials, Login
Name	Protection of Credentials
Requirement	The application shall not divulge in clear text the static authenticator (e.g., password, PIN number, token seed, smart card seed, etc.) of one user to any other user, including administrators.
Use Case(s)	Password Reset, Unlock
Rationale	Passwords shall not be transmitted, stored, or echoed in clear text. Administrators must have the ability to make changes to authentication information, but must not be able to easily impersonate the user.
Priority	Critical/**High**/Medium/Low
Constraints	NA
Comments	Any occurrence of a clear text password, encryption key, or other authentication information in the memory shall be overwritten immediately after use.
Test Case Ref #	STC-ATEN-006

Table 4.12 describes the requirement for password changes.

Table 4.12   Password Changes

Req. ID: SR-ATEN-007	Category: SECURITY
Subcategory(ies)/Tags	Authentication, Credentials, Login, Passwords
Name	Password Changes
Requirement	On first use, the system shall prompt the user to change the initial password and deny access if the user does not comply. Also, it shall allow users to change their own password and/or PIN number later on at any time.
Use Case(s)	First Login to the System, Regular Password Changes
Rationale	This is to prevent the user from relying solely on a default password that is known to administrators. Also, the system must enable individual users to periodically make changes to their authentication information.
Priority	Critical/**High**/Medium/Low
Constraints	NA
Comments	Forcing to change the password during first login will also prevent administrator trying to impersonate the user.
Test Case Ref #	STC-ATEN-007

Table 4.13 describes the requirement for password aging.

Table 4.13   Password Aging

Req. ID: SR-ATEN-008	Category: SECURITY
Subcategory(ies)/Tags	Authentication, Credentials, Login, Passwords
Name	Password Aging
Requirement	The system shall offer a credential aging feature that forces users to periodically change static authentication information. This shall be administrator-configurable.
Use Case(s)	NA

Table 4.13   Password Aging (continued)

Rationale	The periodic aging serves to limit the time period during which a password can be guessed, thus making it more difficult to crack it. In the event that a password is compromised, this also limits the potential use of and damage caused by the compromised password.
Priority	Critical/**High**/Medium/Low
Constraints	To enable ongoing communications between fully automated systems (e.g., batch processing), it is permissible for the system to not require aging under that specific circumstance.
Comments	
Test Case Ref #	STC-ATEN-008

Table 4.14 describes the requirement for password change prompts.

Table 4.14   Password Change Prompt

Req. ID: SR-ATEN-009	Category: SECURITY
Subcategory(ies)/Tags	Authentication, Credentials, Login, Passwords
Name	Password Change Prompt
Requirement	Prior to the expiration of password, the system shall provide notification to the user regarding the imminence of expiration.
Use Case(s)	NA
Rationale	Failure to implement such warning may result in the user's inability to legitimately access the system.
Priority	Critical/High/**Medium**/Low
Constraints	NA
Comments	NA
Test Case Ref #	STC-ATEN-009

Table 4.15 describes the requirement for secure password changes.

Table 4.15 Secure Password Changes

Req. ID: SR-ATEN-010	Category: SECURITY
Subcategory(ies)/Tags	Authentication, Credentials, Login, Passwords
Name	Secure Password Changes
Requirement	The system shall require reauthentication by the user at the time of an attempted change to password or PIN.
Use Case(s)	Password change
Rationale	To make a change to password, it is necessary for the user to be authenticated first, thereby preventing unauthorized changes to passwords.
Priority	Critical/**High**/Medium/Low
Constraints	NA
Comments	NA
Test Case Ref #	STC-ATEN-010

Table 4.16 describes the requirement for preventing password reuse.

Table 4.16 Preventing Password Reuse

Req. ID: SR-ATEN-011	Category: SECURITY
Subcategory(ies)/Tags	Authentication, Credentials, Login, Passwords
Name	Preventing Password Reuse
Requirement	The system shall provide a mechanism to prevent the reuse of passwords within a defined period. For example, when updating a password, a user shall be prevented from using a password that was used in the recent past.
Use Case(s)	Password Change
Rationale	Without this requirement, it is possible for users to alternate between two passwords periodically, making it easier for a third party to obtain unauthorized access to the system, thus defeating the purpose of the password aging feature.

Table 4.16   Preventing Password Reuse (continued)

Priority	Critical/High/**Medium**/Low
Constraints	NA
Comments	NA
Test Case Ref #	STC-ATEN-011

Table 4.17 describes password complexity requirements.

Table 4.17   Password Complexity

Req. ID: SR-ATEN-012	Category: SECURITY
Subcategory(ies)/Tags	Authentication, Credentials, Login
Name	Password Complexity
Requirement	The system shall require that the authentication information is configurable to administrator-specified characteristics for minimum length, alphabetic characters and numeric or special characters.
Use Case(s)	NA
Rationale	Use of trivial and predictable authenticators makes it easier for a third party to obtain an authenticator through brute-force attacks, such as dictionary attacks and other cracking methods.
Priority	Critical/High/**Medium**/Low
Constraints	NA
Comments	NA
Test Case Ref #	STC-ATEN-012

Table 4.18 describes the requirement for Configurable False Acceptance or Rejection.

Table 4.18   Configurable False Accept/Rejection

Req. ID: SR-ATEN-013	Category: SECURITY
Subcategory(ies)/Tags	Authentication, Credentials, Login, Biometrics
Name	Configurable False Accept/Rejection
Requirement	The system shall support administrator-configurable parameters to control false reject and false accept errors on biometric authentication systems.
Use Case(s)	Login
Rationale	The tolerance level for false positives will undoubtedly vary between systems and organizations, so it is necessary to have certain tunable parameters for acceptance/rejection of these cases.
Priority	Critical/**High**/Medium/Low
Constraints	NA
Comments	This has to be set based on organizational requirements, comprehensive testing and risk assessment.
Test Case Ref #	STC-ATEN-013

Table 4.19 describes the requirement for the protection of biometric authentication information.

Table 4.19   Protection of Biometric Authentication Information

Req. ID: SR-ATEN-014	Category: SECURITY
Subcategory(ies)/Tags	Authentication, Credentials, Login, Biometrics
Name	Protection of Biometric Authentication Information

Table 4.19   Protection of Biometric Authentication Information (continued)

Requirement	The system shall take appropriate precautions to protect authentication information while stored. This includes the representation of the user's personal characteristics (e.g., fingerprint, iris pattern).
Use Case(s)	NA
Rationale	Since it may be difficult to forge a personal characteristic of an individual, the typical attack on these systems is against the representation of the biometric on the server. Similarly, since it is nearly impossible to reissue a biometric to a user, it is really critical that the representation of the biometric is adequately secured on the server.
Priority	**Critical**/High/Medium/Low
Constraints	NA
Comments	NA
Test Case Ref #	STC-ATEN-014

4.6   Authorization Requirements

An authorization requirement is any security requirement that specifies the access and usage privileges of authenticated users and client applications.

Table 4.20 describes the requirement for access rights.

Table 4.20   Access Rights

Req. ID: SR-AUTR-001	Category: SECURITY
Subcategory(ies)/Tags	Authorization, Credentials, Access Control
Name	Access Rights
Requirement	The system shall not allow access to system resources without checking the assigned rights and privileges of the authenticated user.
Use Case(s)	Access to different functionalities of the application.

Table 4.20   Access Rights (continued)

Rationale	Authorization is useless unless tied to something that maps identification to rights or privileges. Authorization controls must be applied across all users, resources, and interfaces.
Priority	**Critical**/High/Medium/Low
Constraints	NA
Comments	For a Web application, this would translate to every Web page request having a routine that checks for access rights before processing the request.
Test Case Ref #	STC-AUTR-001-1, STC-AUTR-001-2, STC-AUTR-001-3

Table 4.21 describes the requirement for the protection of biometric authentication information

Table 4.21   Protection of Biometric Authentication Information

Req. ID: SR-AUTR-002	**Category: SECURITY**
Subcategory(ies)/Tags	Authorization, Credentials, Access Control, Biometrics
Name	Protection of Biometric Authentication Information
Requirement	The system shall take appropriate precautions to protect authentication information while stored. This includes the representation of the user's personal characteristics (e.g., fingerprint, iris pattern).
Use Case(s)	NA
Rationale	Since it may be difficult to forge a personal characteristic of an individual, the typical attack on these systems is against the representation of the biometric on the server. Similarly, since it is nearly impossible to reissue a biometric to a user, it is critical that the representation of the biometric is adequately secured on the server.
Priority	**Critical**/High/Medium/Low

Table 4.21   Protection of Biometric Authentication Information (continued)

Constraints	NA
Comments	NA
Test Case Ref #	STC-AUTR-002

Table 4.22 describes the requirement for account lock-outs.

Table 4.22   Account Lock-Out

Req. ID: SR-AUTR-001	Category: SECURITY
Subcategory(ies)/Tags	Authorization, Credentials, Access Control, Authentication, Login
Name	Account Lock-Out
Requirement	If several consecutive incorrect login attempts are made, the system shall generate an alarm and also lock-out the account (for a specified period of time or indefinitely, depending on the criticality of the role and application) after an administrator-specifiable number of attempts. The maximum default setting is three attempts.
Use Case(s)	NA
Rationale	Multiple incorrect logins are often an indication of attempted intrusions. Allowing more than three incorrect attempts can dramatically decrease system security.
Priority	**Critical**/High/Medium/Low
Constraints	NA
Comments	If multiple attempts occur, locking out the account can minimize the threat of unauthorized access, as well as allowing for time to perform forensic analysis of the incident.
Test Case Ref #	STC-AUTR-003

Table 4.23 describes the requirement for login banners.

Table 4.23   Login Banner

Req. ID: SR-AUTR-004	Category: SECURITY
Subcategory(ies)/Tags	Authorization, Credentials, Access Control
Name	Login Banner
Requirement	At the time of login and accessing system resources, the system shall provide the capability to generate an administrator-configurable warning banner. The administrator shall have the capability to create a warning banner that conforms to corporate policy and complies with appropriate national and local laws.
Use Case(s)	Login to the system
Rationale	Warning banners provide legal protection and policy awareness. The lack of ability to create a warning banner can result in liability and lack of legal flexibility (e.g., with respect to prosecution of offenders).
Priority	Critical/High/**Medium**/Low
Constraints	NA
Comments	Similarly, since policies vary between organizations, it is necessary to allow for local customization of the warning banner.
Test Case Ref #	STC-AUTR-004

Table 4.24 describes the requirement for last login information display.

Table 4.24   Last Login Information Display

Req. ID: SR-AUTR-005	Category: SECURITY
Subcategory(ies)/Tags	Authorization, Credentials, Access Control
Name	Last Login Information Display
Requirement	Upon successful session establishment, the system shall display the date and time of the last successful login.
Use Case(s)	Display of post-login home page/screen

Table 4.24 Last Login Information Display (continued)

Rationale	Providing information about a user's last successful login allows a user to determine the existence of an unauthorized login in the past and is useful in detecting possible intrusions.
Priority	Critical/**High**/Medium/Low
Constraints	NA
Comments	In case of Internet-exposed Web apps, displaying the IP address is an additional control.
Test Case Ref #	STC-AUTR-005

Table 4.25 describes the requirement for session timeout.

Table 4.25 Session Timeout

Req. ID: SR-AUTR-006	Category: SECURITY
Subcategory(ies)/Tags	Session Management, Authorization, Authentication
Name	Session Timeout
Requirement	The system shall provide a "timeout" feature so that if during an active session there has not been any exchange of messages across the connection for an administrator-specified period of time, the system shall drop the connection and require a successful reauthentication to regain access.
Use Case(s)	NA
Rationale	Leaving open active sessions increases the possibility of session hijacking as well as disclosure of data.
Priority	**Critical**/High/Medium/Low
Constraints	NA
Comments	NA
Test Case Ref #	STC-AUTR-006

Table 4.26 describes the requirement for access restriction.

Table 4.26   Access Restriction

Req. ID: SR-AUTR-007	Category: SECURITY
Subcategory(ies)/Tags	Authorization, Credentials, Access Control
Name	Access Restriction
Requirement	The system shall have the capability to restrict session establishment based on time-of-day, day-of-week, calendar date of the login, and source of the connection.
Use Case(s)	NA
Rationale	These features enable organizations to enforce more restrictive policies for nonstandard access based on time and location.
Priority	Critical/High/Medium/Low
Constraints	NA
Comments	For Internet-facing Web application, this would include using geo-location information.
Test Case Ref #	STC-AUTR-007

Table 4.27 describes the requirement for user and group privileges.

Table 4.27   User and Group Privileges

Req. ID: SR-AUTR-008	Category: SECURITY
Subcategory(ies)/Tags	Authorization, Credentials, Access Control
Name	User and Group Privileges
Requirement	The system shall have features to assign user and group privileges (i.e., access permissions) to user IDs (not authentication information).
Use Case(s)	NA
Rationale	Assigning user privileges to authenticators may compromise their confidentiality. Instead, assigning privileges to a user enables authorization checking without requiring disclosure of authentication.

Table 4.27   User and Group Privileges (continued)

Priority	Critical/High/Medium/Low
Constraints	NA
Comments	NA
Test Case Ref #	STC-AUTR-008

Table 4.28 describes the requirement for role-based access control.

Table 4.28   Role-Based Access Control

Req. ID: SR-AUTR-009	Category: SECURITY
Subcategory(ies)/Tags	Authorization, Credentials, Access Control
Name	Role-Based Access Control (RBAC)
Requirement	The system shall provide an enforceable mechanism through which users can be segmented into roles (e.g., administrator), involving access to security features and other administrative functions.
Use Case(s)	NA
Rationale	Providing for role-based access control allows individuals to have access based on a specific purpose, rather than just their identity. This minimizes the risk associated with providing super-user or other privileged access to individual users.
Priority	**Critical**/High/Medium/Low
Constraints	NA
Comments	NA
Test Case Ref #	STC-AUTR-009

Table 4.29 describes the requirement for resource control mechanism.

Table 4.29   Resource Control Mechanism

Req. ID: SR-AUTR-001	Category: SECURITY
Subcategory(ies)/Tags	Authorization, Credentials, Access Control
Name	Resource Control Mechanism
Requirement	The system shall provide a resource control mechanism that grants or denies access to a resource based on user and interface privilege.
Use Case(s)	Examples of resources include functions (e.g., backup operation), and data (e.g., files, fields). This covers both the operations- and service-related interfaces.
Rationale	Systems must ensure that user- and role-based access control, as well as interface-based access control, are coordinated, thus allowing for maximum granularity of access control and minimizing the risk of inadvertent "backdoor" access.
Priority	Critical/**High**/Medium/Low
Constraints	NA
Comments	NA
Test Case Ref #	STC-AUTR-002

Table 4.30 describes the requirement for concurrent logon sessions.

Table 4.30   Concurrent logon sessions

Req. ID: SR-AUTR-011	Category: SECURITY
Subcategory(ies)/Tags	Authorization, Credentials, Access Control, Session Management
Name	Concurrent logon sessions
Requirement	The system shall provide the capability for the administrator to specify limits on the number of concurrent logon sessions for a given user, the default value being one.
Use Case(s)	NA

Table 4.30   Concurrent logon sessions (continued)

Rationale	In many situations, there may be a need to restrict concurrent logons for both security and consistency purposes. In some systems, concurrent logins can be used to mask unauthorized activity.
Priority	**Critical**/High/Medium/Low
Constraints	NA
Comments	NA
Test Case Ref #	STC-AUTR-011

4.7   Security Auditing Requirements

A security auditing requirement is any security requirement that specifies the extent to which a business, application, component, or center shall enable security personnel to audit the status and use of its security mechanisms.[4]

Table 4.31 describes the requirement for maintaining an audit log.

Table 4.31   Audit Log

Req. ID: SR-AUDT-001	Category: SECURITY
Subcategory(ies)/Tags	Audit, Forensics, Logging
Name	Audit Log
Requirement	The system shall maintain an audit log that provides adequate information for establishing audit trails on security breaches and user activity.
Use Case(s)	NA
Rationale	The event log is one of the strongest tools in forensic analysis, and can also help determine the root cause of an incident. Additionally, event logs help identify patterns of attack and abnormal behavior.
Priority	**Critical**/High/Medium/Low
Constraints	NA

Table 4.31   Audit Log (continued)

Comments	NA
Test Case Ref #	STC-AUDT-001

Table 4.32 describes the requirement for Logging of Authentication Information

Table 4.32   Logging of Authentication Information

Req. ID: SR-AUDT-002	Category: SECURITY
Subcategory(ies)/Tags	Audit, Forensics, Logging
Name	Logging of Authentication Information
Requirement	The system shall maintain the confidentiality of authenticators (e.g., passwords) by excluding them from being recorded in the audit log.
Use Case(s)	Logs are often visible to persons who are not typically authorized to view authentication information. To enforce the confidentiality of authentication data, as well as the separation of duties requirement, it is necessary to exclude authentication information from audit logs.
Rationale	NA
Priority	**Critical**/High/Medium/Low
Constraints	NA
Comments	NA
Test Case Ref #	STC-AUDT-002

Table 4.33 describes the requirement for logging of specific events

Table 4.33   Logging of Specific Events

Req. ID: SR-AUDT-003	Category: SECURITY
Subcategory(ies)/Tags	Audit, Forensics, Logging
Name	Logging of Specific Events

Table 4.33 Logging of Specific Events (continued)

Requirement	The system shall allow the administrator to configure the audit log to record specified events such as: ■ All sessions established ■ Failed user authentication attempts ■ Unauthorized attempts to access resources (e.g., software, data, process) ■ Administrator actions ■ Administrator disabling of audit logging ■ Events generated (e.g., commands issued) to make changes in users' security profiles and attributes ■ Events generated to make changes in the security profiles and attributes of system interfaces ■ Events generated to make changes in permission levels needed to access a resource ■ Events generated that make changes to the system security configuration ■ Events generated that make modifications to the system software ■ Events generated that make changes to system resources deemed critical (as specified by the administrator).
Use Case(s)	NA
Rationale	All of these events have been deemed to be security-related, since they involve system access, security administration, or event logging. Each of these events can have a significant impact on system security and, if unauthorized, are often signs of an attempted attack or intrusion.
Priority	Critical/**High**/Medium/Low
Constraints	NA
Comments	NA
Test Case Ref #	STC-AUDT-003

Table 4.34 describes the requirement for providing the ability to action on audit log failure

Table 4.34   Action on Audit Log Failure

Req. ID: SR-AUDT-004	Category: SECURITY
Subcategory(ies)/Tags	Audit, Forensics, Logging
Name	Action on Audit Log Failure
Requirement	The system shall provide the administrator the ability to specify the appropriate actions to take (i.e., continue or terminate processing) when the audit log malfunctions or is terminated.
Use Case(s)	
Rationale	Although audit log information could be critical for forensic purposes and for detection of inappropriate or unauthorized activity, the system must allow the administrator to specify whether or not the system should continue to function when the log function is no longer able to perform. Institutions will make this decision based on a risk assessment of the application and the business process.
Priority	Critical/High/**Medium**/Low
Constraints	NA
Comments	NA
Test Case Ref #	STC-AUDT-004

Table 4.35 describes the requirement for archival of audit logs

Table 4.35   Archival of Audit Logs

Req. ID: SR-AUDT-005	Category: SECURITY
Subcategory(ies)/Tags	Audit, Forensics
Name	Archival of Audit Logs
Requirement	The system shall provide the administrator the ability to retrieve, print, and copy (to some long-term storage device) the contents of the audit log.

Table 4.35   Archival of Audit Logs

Use Case(s)	Backup/Archival of Log Files
Rationale	It is desirable to move audit logs to remote systems or storage in order to avoid system failure due to space restrictions, as well as to avoid unauthorized modification. Secondary administrator/operator/auditor roles are needed to allow for log offloading and management without granting broader super-user privileges.
Priority	**Critical**/High/Medium/Low
Constraints	NA
Comments	NA
Test Case Ref #	STC-AUDT-005

Table 4.36 describes the requirement for log review and reporting

Table 4.36   Log Review and Reporting

Req. ID: SR-AUDT-006	Category: SECURITY
Subcategory(ies)/Tags	Audit, Forensics
Name	Log Review and Reporting
Requirement	The system shall provide an administrator with audit analysis tools to selectively retrieve records from the audit log to perform functions such as producing reports, establishing audit trails, etc.
Use Case(s)	NA
Rationale	Audit logs quickly grow very large, making it difficult to get information out of them. This can result in a lack of utility of the log, as well as administrator frustration. Log reduction, search, retrieval tools, and third-party audit management tools provide an easy way to get at relevant data.
Priority	**Critical**/High/Medium/Low
Constraints	NA

Table 4.36   Log Review and Reporting

Comments	NA
Test Case Ref #	STC-AUDT-006

Table 4.37 describes the requirement for logging of specific information

Table 4.37   Logging of Specific Information

Req. ID: SR-AUDT-007	Category: SECURITY
Subcategory(ies)/Tags	Audit, Forensics, Logging
Name	Logging of Specific Information
Requirement	The system shall allow the administrator to configure the audit log to record specified information such as: Date and time of the attempted event Host name of the system generating the log record User ID of the initiator of the attempted event Names of resources accessed Host name of the system that initiated the attempted event Success or failure of the attempt (for the event) Event type
Use Case(s)	NA
Rationale	To properly analyze the impact of an event, it is necessary to have this basic information for use during forensic analysis.
Priority	Critical/**High**/Medium/Low
Constraints	NA
Comments	NA
Test Case Ref #	STC-AUDT-007

Table 4.38 describes the requirement for protection of the audit log.

Table 4.38   Protection of Audit Log

Req. ID: SR-AUDT-008	Category: SECURITY
Subcategory(ies)/Tags	Audit, Forensics, Survivability
Name	Protection of Audit Log
Requirement	The system shall protect the audit log from unauthorized access, modification, or deletion. This protection shall be provided by assigning resource access permission to users and interfaces.
Use Case(s)	NA
Rationale	Since the audit log is important for reconstructing historical activities, it is necessary to protect it from modification. Access to log files should be limited to those with a legitimate business need. An example will be remote logging.
Priority	Critical/High/Medium/Low
Constraints	NA
Comments	NA
Test Case Ref #	STC-AUDT-008

4.8   Confidentiality Requirements

Confidentiality requirements are any security requirements that specify the extent to which an application or component shall ensure that its data and communications is not exposed to unauthorized users.

Table 4.39 describes the requirement for protection of sensitive information.

Table 4.39   Sensitive Information Protection

Req. ID: SR-CONF-001	Category: SECURITY
Subcategory(ies)/Tags	Confidentiality, Data Protection, Information Disclosure, Integrity
Name	Sensitive Information Protection

Table 4.39   Sensitive Information Protection (continued)

Requirement	The system shall have the capability to protect system-defined, security-related, and user-defined selected information from unauthorized disclosure while it is stored or in transit.
Use Case(s)	NA
Rationale	Information related to security, if disclosed, can lead to unauthorized access to systems, disclosure of sensitive transaction and system information, and loss of integrity. In addition to system-defined sensitive information, it is also important to protect user-defined sensitive information using similar mechanisms.
Priority	**Critical**/High/Medium/Low
Constraints	NA
Comments	NA
Test Case Ref #	STC-CONF-001

Table 4.40 describes the requirement for securing cryptographic keys.

Table 4.40   Cryptographic Key Security

Req. ID: SR-CONF-002	**Category: SECURITY**
Subcategory(ies)/Tags	Confidentiality, Data Protection, Information Disclosure, Cryptographic Keys
Name	Cryptographic Key Security
Requirement	If cryptographic keys are generated and stored, the system shall provide secure key storage that is impractical to compromise through a logical or physical attack.
Use Case(s)	NA
Rationale	Keys provide the fundamental core to cryptographic protection, and their disclosure severely compromises confidentiality of data. Systems must provide key protection commensurate with the key's purpose.
Priority	**Critical**/High/Medium/Low

Table 4.40   Cryptographic Key Security (continued)

Constraints	NA
Comments	NA
Test Case Ref #	STC-CONF-002

Table 4.41 describes the requirement for secure generation of cryptographic keys.

Table 4.41   Cryptographic Key Strength

Req. ID: SR-CONF-003	Category: SECURITY
Subcategory(ies)/Tags	Confidentiality, Data Protection, Information Disclosure, Cryptographic Keys
Name	Cryptographic Key Strength
Requirement	If cryptographic keys are generated, the system shall implement a standard key generation algorithm that generates non-predictable values.
Use Case(s)	NA
Rationale	A cryptographic algorithm is only as strong as the strength of the key generation algorithm. This has proven to be the source of security breaches and vulnerabilities.
Priority	**Critical**/High/Medium/Low
Constraints	NA
Comments	NA
Test Case Ref #	STC-CONF-003

Table 4.42 describes the requirement for cryptographic key expiration.

Table 4.42   Cryptographic Key Expiration

Req. ID: SR-CONF-004	Category: SECURITY
Subcategory(ies)/Tags	Confidentiality, Data Protection, Information Disclosure, Cryptographic Keys
Name	Cryptographic Key Expiration

Table 4.42   Cryptographic Key Expiration (continued)

Requirement	The system shall have the capability to enforce the administrator-specified time period for the validity of keys for a particular use and/or user and shall prevent further use of a key after it has expired.
Use Case(s)	NA
Rationale	The duration of key validity is directly proportional to the risk of compromise. Key validity periods also provide the ability to enforce local policies and procedures. Key validity periods must be enforced by the relying party and at the point of issuance of the certificate. Due to caching and the vagaries of individual copies, it is not sufficient to enforce key validity solely at the sending party's end.
Priority	**Critical**/High/Medium/Low
Constraints	NA
Comments	NA
Test Case Ref #	STC-CONF-004

Table 4.43 describes the requirement for cryptographic key revocation.

Table 4.43   Cryptographic Key Revocation

Req. ID: SR-CONF-005	Category: SECURITY
Subcategory(ies)/Tags	Confidentiality, Data Protection, Information Disclosure, Cryptographic Keys
Name	Cryptographic Key Revocation
Requirement	The system shall have the capability to enforce the immediate revocation of a user and the associated keying material when requested by the administrator.
Use Case(s)	NA

Table 4.43   Cryptographic Key Revocation (continued)

Rationale	Revocation is necessary to enforce policy. Since all keys can be cached locally, the only way to prevent use of an unauthorized key or certificate is to globally denote revocation of that key or certificate.
Priority	**Critical**/High/Medium/Low
Constraints	NA
Comments	NA
Test Case Ref #	STC-CONF-005

Table 4.44 describes the requirement for cryptographic key recovery.

Table 4.44   Cryptographic Key Recovery

Req. ID: SR-CONF-006	**Category: SECURITY**
Subcategory(ies)/Tags	Confidentiality, Data Protection, Information Disclosure, Cryptographic Keys
Name	Cryptographic Key Recovery
Requirement	The system shall support recovery of all encryption keys by an authorized and authenticated user.
Use Case(s)	NA
Rationale	It must be possible to recover a key in the event that the key's owner or primary caretaker is unable to provide the key for legitimate use (e.g., the key has been lost; the individual has left the company).
Priority	**Critical**/High/Medium/Low
Constraints	NA
Comments	NA
Test Case Ref #	STC-CONF-006

Table 4.45 describes another requirement for securing signing keys.

Table 4.45   Signing Key Security

Req. ID: SR-CONF-007	Category: SECURITY
Subcategory(ies)/Tags	Confidentiality, Data Protection, Information Disclosure, Cryptographic Keys, Digital Signature
Name	Signing Key Security
Requirement	The system shall not use signing keys for purposes of data encryption.
Use Case(s)	NA
Rationale	In conjunction with the requirement for key recovery in SR-39 (above), it is necessary to separate encryption keys, which must be recoverable, from signing keys, which identify the owner and must not be recoverable.
Priority	**Critical**/High/Medium/Low
Constraints	NA
Comments	NA
Test Case Ref #	STC-CONF-007

Table 4.46 describes the requirement for securing signing keys from third parties.

Table 4.46   Security of Signing Keys

Req. ID: SR-CONF-008	Category: SECURITY
Subcategory(ies)/Tags	Confidentiality, Data Protection, Information Disclosure, Cryptographic Keys
Name	Security of Signing Keys
Requirement	The system shall not allow for the third-party recovery of keys used to create digital signatures.
Use Case(s)	NA

Table 4.46   Security of Signing Keys (continued)

Rationale	Nonrepudiation requires that any keying material be maintained in a secure fashion and not shared outside of the authorized administrative controls
Priority	**Critical**/High/Medium/Low
Constraints	NA
Comments	NA
Test Case Ref #	STC-CONF-008

4.9   Integrity Requirements

An integrity requirement is any security requirement that specifies the extent to which an application or component shall ensure that its data and communications are not intentionally corrupted via unauthorized creation, modification, or deletion.[4]

Table 4.47 describes the requirement for integrity checking.

Table 4.47   Integrity Checking

Req. ID: SR-INTG-001	Category: SECURITY
Subcategory(ies)/Tags	Data Integrity, Data Protection
Name	Integrity Checking
Requirement	The system shall provide secure integrity-checking capabilities through the interface between the user and the system and among systems.
Use Case(s)	NA
Rationale	It is necessary to ensure the validity of transmission between systems (i.e., to ensure that the data received is the same as that which was sent). In the event that the communication is over a network or via a location in memory or disk, this validity can be provided through various tools. If the data is on the same system, then a protected path is required.
Priority	Critical/**High**/Medium/Low

Table 4.47   Integrity Checking (continued)

Constraints	NA
Comments	NA
Test Case Ref #	STC-INTG-001

Table 4.48 describes the requirement for source identification.

Table 4.48   Source Identification

Req. ID: SR-INTG-002	Category: SECURITY
Subcategory(ies)/Tags	Data Integrity, Data Protection, Audit
Name	Source Identification
Requirement	The system shall have the capability to propagate, when requested, the original user identifier to the destination.
Use Case(s)	NA
Rationale	The source identification should be available to further back-end systems for audit purposes.
Priority	Critical/High/**Medium**/Low
Constraints	NA
Comments	NA
Test Case Ref #	STC-INTG-002

Table 4.49 describes the requirement for preserving header integrity.

Table 4.49   Header Integrity

Req. ID: SR-INTG-003	Category: SECURITY
Subcategory(ies)/Tags	Data Integrity, Data Protection
Name	Header Integrity
Requirement	The system shall provide mechanisms to preserve the integrity of protocol header information and user data.
Use Case(s)	NA

Table 4.49   Header Integrity

Rationale	Data integrity should not merely be limited to message content, but should also be applied to general packet header information and routing information. Lack of header integrity mechanisms creates opportunity for spoofing and masquerading.
Priority	**Critical**/High/Medium/Low
Constraints	NA
Comments	NA
Test Case Ref #	STC-INTG-003

Table 4.50 describes the requirement for protecting against replay attacks.

Table 4.50   Replay Attack Protection

Req. ID: SR-INTG-004	Category: SECURITY
Subcategory(ies)/Tags	Data Integrity, Data Protection, Immunity
Name	Replay Attack Protection
Requirement	The system shall provide mechanisms to detect communication security violations in real-time, such as replay attacks that duplicate an authentic message.
Use Case(s)	NA
Rationale	Serious attacks on data integrity, such as replay, represent a significant threat to system security and need to be dealt with as soon as possible.
Priority	**Critical**/High/Medium/Low
Constraints	NA
Comments	NA
Test Case Ref #	STC-INTG-004

Table 4.51 describes the requirement for integrity of sensitive information.

Table 4.51   Integrity of Sensitive Information

Req. ID: SR-INTG-005	Category: SECURITY
Subcategory(ies)/Tags	Data Integrity, Data Protection
Name	Integrity of Sensitive Information
Requirement	The system shall support protocols that bind the integrity of sensitive information with the integrity of the associated protocol information.
Use Case(s)	NA
Rationale	Integrity of network data (e.g., protocol headers) should be tied to integrity of packet data, to further ensure the integrity of the transmission.
Priority	**Critical**/High/Medium/Low
Constraints	NA
Comments	NA
Test Case Ref #	STC-INTG-005

Table 4.52 describes the requirement for protecting the integrity of logs.

Table 4.52   Integrity of Logs

Req. ID: SR-INTG-006	Category: SECURITY
Subcategory(ies)/Tags	Data Integrity, Data Protection, Logging
Name	Integrity of Logs
Requirement	The system shall have the capability to protect the integrity of audit log records by generating integrity checks (e.g., checksums or secure hashes) when the log records are created, and by verifying the integrity check data when the record is accessed.
Use Case(s)	NA
Rationale	A common technique, as part of an attack, is to alter the log and audit records on a system to hide unauthorized activity. Integrity checks on these records can help prevent such activity.

Table 4.52   Integrity of Logs (continued)

Priority	**Critical**/High/Medium/Low
Constraints	NA
Comments	NA
Test Case Ref #	STC-INTG-006

Table 4.53 describes the requirement for providing the capabilities of integrity checking.

Table 4.53   Integrity Checks

Req. ID: SR-INTG-007	Category: SECURITY
Subcategory(ies)/Tags	Data Integrity, Data Protection
Name	Integrity Checks
Requirement	The system shall have the capability to protect data integrity by performing data integrity checks and reject the data if the integrity check fails.
Use Case(s)	▪ Verification of message authentication code (MAC), keyed Hash Message Authentication Code (HCAC) or digital signature ▪ Adequate alert messages in response to potentially damaging commands before execution ▪ Proper handling of duplicate and multiple inputs ▪ Proper handling of securely generated encryption keying information ▪ Proper handling of overflow conditions
Rationale	Data integrity is a large issue, and threats take many forms. The system should take steps to ensure that the integrity of data is maintained at all relevant points.
Priority	**Critical**/High/Medium/Low
Constraints	NA

Table 4.53 Integrity Checks (continued)

Comments	NA
Test Case Ref #	STC-INTG-007

4.10 Availability Requirements

An availability requirement is any security requirement that specifies the extent to which an application or system shall maintain uptime and be available to all its authorized users. Some availability requirements are also found in the chapters related to application and infrastructure resilience.

Table 4.54 describes the requirement for secure scalability.

Table 4.54 Secure Scalability

Req. ID: SR-AVAL-001	Category: SECURITY
Subcategory(ies)/Tags	Scalability, Performance, Availability
Name	Secure Scalability
Requirement	The system shall be able to continue to operate securely when various operating parameters increase or decrease.
Use Case(s)	NA
Rationale	Since performance of products varies greatly from one environment to the next, and since scalability can be measured with respect to a number of parameters, the only scalability tests conducted under this framework will be a verification of vendor claims regarding the scalability of the product, and claims that security features (and, if applicable, functionality) remain consistent at those levels.
Priority	Critical/High/Medium/Low
Constraints	NA
Comments	NA
Test Case Ref #	STC-AVAL-001

Table 4.55 describes the requirement for capability to monitor availability.

Table 4.55   Capability to Monitor Availability

Req. ID: SR-AVAL-002	Category: SECURITY
Subcategory(ies)/Tags	System Integrity, System Maintenance, Availability
Name	Capability to Monitor Availability
Requirement	The system shall provide an administrator with the capability to monitor the state of availability of critical system resources (e.g., overflow indication, lost messages, and buffer queues).
Use Case(s)	NA
Rationale	To properly ensure that a system is functioning properly, it is necessary for the administrator to be able to monitor system metrics that affect normal operations.
Priority	Critical/**High**/Medium/Low
Constraints	NA
Comments	NA
Test Case Ref #	STC-AVAL-002

4.11   Nonrepudiation Requirements

A nonrepudiation requirement is any security requirement that specifies the extent to which a business, application, or component shall prevent a party to one of its interactions (e.g., message, transaction) from denying having participated in all or part of the interaction.[4]

Table 4.56 describes the requirement for secure logging of specific information

Table 4.56   Secure Logging of Specific Information

Req. ID: SR-NREP-001	Category: SECURITY
Subcategory(ies)/Tags	Nonrepudiation, Logging, Accountability
Name	Secure Logging of Specific Information

Table 4.56   Secure Logging of Specific Information (continued)

Requirement	The system shall have the capability to securely record information related to the reception of specific information from a user or another system.
Use Case(s)	NA
Rationale	To properly enforce nonrepudiation, it is necessary to properly document receipt of all data.
Priority	**Critical**/High/Medium/Low
Constraints	NA
Comments	NA
Test Case Ref #	STC-NREP-001

Table 4.57 describes the requirement for time stamping of messages

Table 4.57   Time Stamping

Req. ID: SR-NREP-002	Category: SECURITY
Subcategory(ies)/Tags	Nonrepudiation, Logging, Accountability
Name	Time Stamping
Requirement	The system shall have the capability to securely link received information with the originator of the information and other characteristics such as time and date.
Use Case(s)	NA
Rationale	To enforce nonepudiation, it is necessary to tie specific data to a user or system, as well as to the time at which it was sent. This supports accountability of actions and is a core concept of non-repudiation.
Priority	Critical/High/Medium/Low
Constraints	NA
Comments	NA
Test Case Ref #	STC-NREP-002

Table 4.58 describes the requirement for digital signatures

Table 4.58   Digital Signatures

Req. ID: SR-NREP-003	Category: SECURITY
Subcategory(ies)/Tags	Nonrepudiation, Logging, Accountability, Digital Signatures, Cryptographic Keys
Name	Digital Signatures
Requirement	The system shall have the capability to interface with a specified trusted third party to obtain cryptographic keys that will link the received information or request with a specific user.
Use Case(s)	NA
Rationale	Digital signatures are often used to provide nonrepudiation. In order to properly verify a signature, it may be necessary to obtain verification from a third party, such as a certification authority, validation authority, or certificate directory.
Priority	Critical/**High**/Medium/Low
Constraints	NA
Comments	NA
Test Case Ref #	STC-NREP-003

4.12   Immunity Requirements

An immunity requirement is any security requirement that specifies the extent to which an application or component shall protect itself from infection by unauthorized undesirable programs (e.g., computer viruses, worms, and Trojan horses).

Table 4.59 describes the default denial requirements.

Table 4.59   Default Deny

Req. ID: SR-IMMU-001	Category: SECURITY
Subcategory(ies)/Tags	Authorization, Credentials, Access Control, Immunity
Name	Default Deny

Table 4.59   Default Deny (continued)

Requirement	The system shall deny the access unless a user has permission to access a resource.
Use Case(s)	NA
Rationale	By default, systems must take a "closed" approach to access control. This minimizes the possibility of "backdoor" unauthorized access to a system.
Priority	**Critical**/High/Medium/Low
Constraints	NA
Comments	NA
Test Case Ref #	STC-IMMU-001

Table 4.60 describes the requirement for scope limitation.

Table 4.60   Scope Limitation

Req. ID: SR-IMMU-002	Category: SECURITY
Subcategory(ies)/Tags	Authorization, Credentials, Access Control, Immunity
Name	Scope Limitation
Requirement	The system shall provide the ability to define system level or administrative privileges with appropriate scope limitations.
Use Case(s)	NA
Rationale	Many systems provide privileged access without any compensating controls or scope limitations, increasing the risk of damage from a rogue administrator or privileged user. For example, after initiating an administrator session, the system could provide the ability to restrict access to operational or regular end-user functions.
Priority	**Critical**/High/Medium/Low
Constraints	NA

Table 4.60   Scope Limitation (continued)

Comments	NA
Test Case Ref #	STC-IMMU-002

Table 4.61 describes the requirement to limit execution of potentially damaging commands.

Table 4.61   Limit Execution

Req. ID: SR-IMMU-003	Category: SECURITY
Subcategory(ies)/Tags	Authorization, Credentials, Access Control, Immunity
Name	Limit Execution
Requirement	The system shall have the capability to prevent access to potentially damaging commands (e.g., delete all files) from users who do not need to execute such commands on a regular basis and from interfaces that are not intended to be used for such commands.
Use Case(s)	NA
Rationale	Limiting execution of damaging system commands can prevent damage (intentional or otherwise) to the system.
Priority	**Critical**/High/Medium/Low
Constraints	NA
Comments	NA
Test Case Ref #	STC-IMMU-003

Table 4.62 describes the requirement for Create, Read, Update, and Delete (CRUD)–based access control.

Table 4.62   CRUD-Based Access Control

Req. ID: SR-IMMU-004	Category: SECURITY
Subcategory(ies)/Tags	Authorization, Credentials, Access Control, Immunity

Table 4.62   CRUD-Based Access Control (continued)

Name	CRUD-Based Access Control
Requirement	The system shall have the capability to impose access control on the basis of functions such as Create, Read, Update, and Delete (CRUD).
Use Case(s)	NA
Rationale	Access to system resources must be restricted in a manner that allows for granularity in accordance with organizational policy.
Priority	Critical/**High**/Medium/Low
Constraints	NA
Comments	NA
Test Case Ref #	STC-IMMU-004

4.13   Survivability Requirements

A survivability requirement is any security requirement that specifies the extent to which an application or center shall survive the intentional loss or destruction of a component.[4]

Table 4.63 describes the requirement for buffer overflow protection.

Table 4.63   Buffer Overflow Protection

Req. ID: SR-SURV-001	Category: SECURITY
Subcategory(ies)/Tags	System Integrity, System Maintenance, Survivability
Name	Buffer Overflow Protection
Requirement	The system shall prevent buffer overflow conditions that allow for unauthorized access.
Use Case(s)	
Rationale	Buffer overflow conditions are a common source of unauthorized access to systems, allowing for an unauthorized user to cause a system to execute a (potentially damaging) command.

Table 4.63   Buffer Overflow Protection (continued)

Priority	**Critical**/High/Medium/Low
Constraints	NA
Comments	NA
Test Case Ref #	STC-SURV-001

Table 4.64 describes the requirement for log malfunction alerting.

Table 4.64   Log Malfunction Alert

Req. ID: SR-SURV-002	Category: SECURITY
Subcategory(ies)/Tags	Audit, Forensics, Survivability
Name	Log Malfunction Alert
Requirement	The system shall generate a real-time alarm and have the capability to send an e-mail notification for impeding failures (running out of storage space) or if the audit log malfunctions is shut down for any reason.
Use Case(s)	NA
Rationale	If the audit log malfunctions, there is no way to track activities or transactions. This makes it difficult to conduct business under normal operations. Rather than shutting down the system, most organizations choose to operate under some form of emergency circumstances. To inform the organization of the need to invoke these new operational procedures and to begin to address the problem at hand, there is a need to sound a real-time alarm and send an e-mail notification (since real-time alarms to the console are typically ignored by the operators).
Priority	Critical/High/**Medium**/Low
Constraints	NA
Comments	NA
Test Case Ref #	STC-SURV-002

Table 4.65 describes the requirement for logging through system restarts.

Table 4.65   Logging through System Restarts

Req. ID: SR-SURV-003	Category: SECURITY
Subcategory(ies)/Tags	Data Integrity, Audit, Forensics, Logging, Survivability
Name	Logging through System Restarts
Requirement	The system shall allow the audit log and its control mechanisms to maintain integrity and completeness through system restarts.
Use Case(s)	
Rationale	System restarts must not clear the log. Since a shutdown or restart can be associated with a security-related event (or even be one on its own), it is necessary for logs to note them as an event and to resume normal operations upon restart.
Priority	**Critical**/High/Medium/Low
Constraints	NA
Comments	NA
Test Case Ref #	STC-SURV-003

4.14   Systems Maintenance Security Requirements

A system maintenance security requirement is any security requirement that specifies the extent to which an application, component, or center shall prevent authorized modifications (e.g., defect fixes, enhancements, updates, restarts, restores, etc.) from accidentally defeating its security mechanisms.

Table 4.66 describes the requirement for source tracking.

Table 4.66   Source Tracking

Req. ID: SR-SYSM-001	Category: SECURITY
Subcategory(ies)/Tags	System Integrity, System Maintenance, Forensics
Name	Source Tracking

Table 4.66   Source Tracking (continued)

Requirement	For software and data created or modified in the system, the system shall provide an administrator with the capability to retrieve the user ID along with the date and time associated with that creation or modification.
Use Case(s)	NA
Rationale	To ensure that no unauthorized modifications are made to the system, and to support forensic analysis of suspected events, it must be possible for an administrator to track the source of individual events such as this.
Priority	**Critical**/High/Medium/Low
Constraints	NA
Comments	NA
Test Case Ref #	STC-SYSM-001

Table 4.67 describes the requirement for system integrity checks.

Table 4.67   System Integrity Checks

Req. ID: SR-SYSM-002	Category: SECURITY
Subcategory(ies)/Tags	System Integrity, System Maintenance
Name	System Integrity Checks
Requirement	The system shall provide an administrator with the capability to perform integrity checks (e.g., synchronization points, checksums) on system data and software.
Use Case(s)	NA
Rationale	To proactively prevent unauthorized system modification, the administrator must be able to conduct periodic checks on the integrity system's data and software.
Priority	Critical/**High**/Medium/Low
Constraints	NA

Table 4.67   System Integrity Checks

Comments	NA
Test Case Ref #	STC-SYSM-002

Table 4.68 describes the requirement for system snapshot reporting.

Table 4.68   System Snapshot Report

Req. ID: SR-SYSM-003	Category: SECURITY
Subcategory(ies)/Tags	System Integrity, System Maintenance
Name	System Snapshot Report
Requirement	The system shall provide the administrator with the capability to generate a system snapshot report detailing the values of the parameters and flags that affect secure operation of the system.
Use Case(s)	NA
Rationale	To properly maintain the system and its performance from both an operational and a security perspective, it is necessary to determine the current security "snapshot" of the system.
Priority	Critical/**High**/Medium/Low
Constraints	NA
Comments	NA
Test Case Ref #	STC-SYSM-003

Table 4.69 describes the requirement for secure system recovery.

Table 4.69   Secure Recovery

Req. ID: SR-SYSM-004	Category: SECURITY
Subcategory(ies)/Tags	System Integrity, System Maintenance
Name	Secure Recovery
Requirement	The system shall provide an administrator with the capability to perform secure recovery.
Use Case(s)	

Table 4.69   Secure Recovery (continued)

Rationale	In the event of a system crash or shutdown, system performance becomes unpredictable. It is imperative that the administrator be able to reconstruct the system according to security policy and good practices. Therefore, it is necessary to have a trusted security "baseline" configuration from which to restore.
Priority	Critical/High/Medium/Low
Constraints	NA
Comments	NA
Test Case Ref #	STC-SYSM-004

Table 4.70 describes the requirement for security data backup and restore.

Table 4.70   Security Data Backup/Restore

Req. ID: SR-SYSM-005	Category: SECURITY
Subcategory(ies)/Tags	System Integrity, System Maintenance
Name	Security Data Backup/Restore
Requirement	The system shall provide an administrator with the capability to back up and restore all security-relevant data, such as system configurations, user profiles, and access permissions.
Use Case(s)	NA
Rationale	In the event of a system crash or shutdown, system performance becomes unpredictable. It is always necessary that the administrator be able to reconstruct the system according to security policy and good practices. Therefore, it is necessary to have a trusted security "baseline" configuration from which to restore.
Priority	Critical/**High**/Medium/Low
Constraints	NA

Table 4.70   Security Data Backup/Restore (continued)

Comments	NA
Test Case Ref #	STC-SYSM-005

Table 4.71 describes the requirement for checking the integrity of security data from backup sources.

Table 4.71   Restore from Backup Checks

Req. ID: SR-SYSM-006	Category: SECURITY
Subcategory(ies)/Tags	System Integrity, System Maintenance
Name	Restore from Backup Checks
Requirement	The system shall have the capability to check the integrity of security data read from a backup file when performing a restore function.
Use Case(s)	NA
Rationale	In the event of a system crash or shutdown, system performance becomes unpredictable. It is always imperative that the administrator be able to reconstruct the system according to security policy and good practices. Therefore, it is necessary to have a trusted security "baseline" configuration from which to restore.
Priority	Critical/High/Medium/Low
Constraints	NA
Comments	NA
Test Case Ref #	STC-SYSM-006

Table 4.72 describes the requirement for security setting recovery.

Table 4.72   Security Settings Recovery

Req. ID: SR-SYSM-007	Category: SECURITY
Subcategory(ies)/Tags	System Integrity, System Maintenance
Name	Security Settings Recovery

Table 4.72   Security Settings Recovery (continued)

Requirement	The system shall securely recover all of the security settings and stored security parameters during the normal recovery operation.
Use Case(s)	NA
Rationale	When the system supports recovery of security settings across system invocations, the benefits are efficiency and consistency. Consistency of security settings is particularly important, because change always creates the potential for error. When the system recovers the security settings, the administrator is not forced to perform actions that could lead to errors and thus security breaches.
Priority	Critical/**High**/Medium/Low
Constraints	NA
Comments	NA
Test Case Ref #	STC-SYSM-007

Table 4.73 describes the requirement for retaining security parameters through system restarts.

Table 4.73   Security Parameters through System Restarts

Req. ID: SR-SYSM-008	Category: SECURITY
Subcategory(ies)/Tags	System Integrity, System Maintenance
Name	Security Parameters through System Restarts
Requirement	The system shall retain the existing security parameters even after a restart or recovery.
Use Case(s)	
Rationale	For example, user IDs and passwords that have been assigned to the users shall not revert to a vendor-delivered default such as system/system or admin/admin.
Priority	Critical/High/Medium/Low
Constraints	NA

Table 4.73   Security Parameters through System Restarts (continued)

Comments	NA
Test Case Ref #	STC-SYSM-008

4.15   Privacy Requirements

A privacy requirement is any security requirement that specifies the extent to which a business, application, component, or center shall provide provisions to exercise the rights and obligations of individuals and organizations with respect to the collection, use, retention, disclosure, and disposal of personal information.

Table 4.74 describes the requirement for personal information identification and classification.

Table 4.74   Personal Information Identification and Classification

Req. ID: SR-PRIV-001	Category: SECURITY
Subcategory(ies)/Tags	Privacy, Management, Information Classification
Name	Personal Information Identification and Classification
Requirement	The system shall identify the types of personal information and sensitive personal information and the related processes, systems, and third parties involved in the handling of such information.

Use Case(s)	The entity has to have both an information classification policy and process, which include the following:
	■ A classification process, which identifies and classifies information into one or more of the following categories:
	  ■ Business confidential
	  ■ Personal information (sensitive and other personal information)
	  ■ Business general
	  ■ Public

Table 4.74   Personal Information Identification and Classification (continued)

Use Case(s)	▪ Identifying processes, systems, and third parties that handle personal information ▪ Specific security and privacy policies and procedures that apply to each category of information
Rationale	The first principle of the Generally Accepted Privacy Principles (GAPP) is Management. This principle requires that the entity define, document, communicate, and assign accountability for its privacy policies and procedures.
Priority	Critical/**High**/Medium/Low
Constraints	NA
Comments	All such information is covered by the entity's privacy and related security policies and procedures.

Table 4.75 describes the requirement for disallowing use of private information in test and development

Table 4.75   Disallow Use of Private Information in Test and Development

Req. ID: SR-PRIV-002	Category: SECURITY
Subcategory(ies)/Tags	Privacy, Management
Name	Disallow Use of Private information in Test and Development
Requirement	The use of personal information in process and system test and development is prohibited unless such information is anonymized or otherwise protected in accordance with the entity's privacy policies and procedures.
Use Case(s)	NA
Rationale	Changes to system components have to minimize the risk of any adverse effect on the protection of personal information (accidental and intentional disclosure from test and development systems), so all test data are to be anonymized.

Table 4.75   Disallow Use of Private Information in Test and Development

Priority	Critical/**High**/Medium/Low
Constraints	NA
Comments	NA

Table 4.76 describes the requirement for provision of notice.

Table 4.76   Provision of Notice

Req. ID: SR-PRIV-003	Category: SECURITY
Subcategory(ies)/Tags	Privacy, Notice
Name	Provision of Notice
Requirement	Notice is provided to the individual about the entity's privacy policies and procedures (1) at or before the time personal information is collected, or as soon as practical thereafter, (2) at or before the entity changes its privacy policies and procedures, or as soon as practical thereafter, or (3) before personal information is used for new purposes not previously identified.
Use Case(s)	The privacy notice has to be
	▪ Readily accessible and available when personal information is first collected from the individual.
	▪ Provided in a timely manner (that is, at or before the time personal information is collected, or as soon as practical thereafter) to enable individuals to decide whether or not to submit personal information to the entity.
	▪ Clearly dated to allow individuals to determine whether the notice has changed since the last time they read it or since the last time they submitted personal information to the entity.

Table 4.76   Provision of Notice

Rationale	The second principle of the Generally Accepted Privacy Principles (GAPP) is Notice. This principle requires that the entity provide notice about its privacy policies and procedures and identify the purpose for which personal information is collected, used, retained, and disclosed.
Priority	Critical/**High**/Medium/Low
Constraints	NA
Comments	Some regulatory requirements indicate that a privacy notice is to be provided on a periodic basis, for example, annually in the Gramm-Leach-Bliley Act (GLBA).

Table 4.77 describes the requirement for communication to individuals.

Table 4.77   Communication to Individuals

Req. ID: SR-PRIV-004	Category: SECURITY
Subcategory(ies)/Tags	Privacy, Choice and Consent
Name	Communication to Individuals
Requirement	Individuals are informed (1) about the choices available to them with respect to the collection, use, and disclosure of personal information, and (2) that implicit or explicit consent is required to collect, use, and disclose personal information, unless a law or regulation specifically requires or allows otherwise.

Table 4.77 Communication to Individuals (continued)

Use Case(s)	The entity's privacy notice describes, in a clear and concise manner, the following:
	▪ The choices available to the individual regarding the collection, use, and disclosure of personal information
	▪ The process an individual should follow to exercise these choices (for example, checking an opt-out box to decline receiving marketing materials)
	▪ The ability of, and process for, an individual to change contact preferences
	The consequences of failing to provide personal information required for a transaction or service
Rationale	The third principle of the Generally Accepted Privacy Principles (GAPP) is Choice and Consent. This principle requires that the entity describe the choices available to the individual and obtain implicit or explicit consent with respect to the collection, use, and disclosure of personal information.
Priority	Critical/**High**/Medium/Low
Constraints	NA
Comments	NA

Table 4.78 describes the requirement for implicit or explicit consent.

Table 4.78 Implicit or Explicit Consent

Req. ID: SR-PRIV-005	Category: SECURITY
Subcategory(ies)/Tags	Privacy, Choice and Consent
Name	Implicit or Explicit Consent
Requirement	Implicit or explicit consent is obtained from the individual at or before the time personal information is collected or soon after. The individual's preferences expressed in his or her consent are confirmed and implemented.

Table 4.78 Implicit or Explicit Consent (continued)

Use Case(s)	The entity:
	■ Obtains and documents an individual's consent in a timely manner (that is, at or before the time personal information is collected or soon after)
	■ Confirms an individual's preferences (in writing or electronically)
	■ Documents and manages changes to an individual's preferences
	■ Ensures that an individual's preferences are implemented in a timely fashion
	■ Addresses conflicts in the records about an individual's preferences by providing a process for users to notify and challenge a vendor's interpretation of their contact preferences
	■ Ensures that the use of personal information, throughout the entity and by third parties, is in accordance with an individual's preferences.
Rationale	The third principle of the Generally Accepted Privacy Principles (GAPP) is Choice and Consent. This principle requires that the entity describe the choices available to the individual and obtain implicit or explicit consent with respect to the collection, use, and disclosure of personal information.
Priority	Critical/**High**/Medium/Low
Constraints	NA
Comments	NA

Table 4.79 describes the requirement for explicit consent for sensitive information.

Table 4.79 Explicit Consent for Sensitive Information

Req. ID: SR-PRIV-006	Category: SECURITY
Subcategory(ies)/Tags	Privacy, Choice and Consent

Table 4.79   Explicit Consent for Sensitive Information (continued)

Name	Explicit Consent for Sensitive Information
Requirement	Explicit consent is obtained directly from the individual when sensitive personal information is collected, used, or disclosed, unless a law or regulation specifically requires otherwise.
Use Case(s)	The entity collects sensitive information only if the individual provides explicit consent. Explicit consent requires that the individual affirmatively agree, through some action, to the use or disclosure of the sensitive information. Explicit consent is obtained directly from the individual and documented, for example, by requiring the individual to check a box or sign a form. This is sometimes referred to as opt in.
Rationale	The third principle of the Generally Accepted Privacy Principles (GAPP) is Choice and Consent. This principle requires that the entity describe the choices available to the individual and obtain implicit or explicit consent with respect to the collection, use, and disclosure of personal information.
Priority	Critical/**High**/Medium/Low
Constraints	NA
Comments	Some jurisdictions consider government-issued personal identifiers, for example, Social Security numbers or Social Insurance numbers, to be sensitive information.

Table 4.80 describes the requirement for consent for online data transfers.

Table 4.80   Consent for Online Data Transfers

Req. ID: SR-PRIV-007	Category: SECURITY
Subcategory(ies)/Tags	Privacy, Choice and Consent
Name	Consent for Online Data Transfers

Table 4.80   Consent for Online Data Transfers (continued)

Requirement	Consent is obtained before personal information is transferred to or from an individual's computer or other similar device.
Use Case(s)	The entity requests customer permission to store, alter, or copy personal information (other than cookies) in the customer's computer or other similar electronic device.
	If the customer has indicated to the entity that it does not want cookies, the entity has controls to ensure that cookies are not stored on the customer's computer or other similar electronic device.
	Entities will not download software that will transfer personal information without obtaining permission.
Rationale	The third principle of the Generally Accepted Privacy Principles (GAPP) is Choice and Consent. This principle requires that the entity describe the choices available to the individual and obtain implicit or explicit consent with respect to the collection, use, and disclosure of personal information.
Priority	Critical/**High**/Medium/Low
Constraints	NA
Comments	Consideration should be given to prevent or detect the introduction of software that is designed to mine or extract information from a computer or other similar electronic device and therefore may be used to extract personal information, for example, spyware.

Table 4.81 describes the requirement for communication to individuals.

Table 4.81   Communication to Individuals

Req. ID: SR-PRIV-008	Category: SECURITY
Subcategory(ies)/Tags	Privacy, Collection
Name	Communication to Individuals

Table 4.81   Communication to Individuals (continued)

Requirement	Individuals are informed that personal information is collected only for the purposes identified in the notice. The types of personal information collected and the methods of collection, including the use of cookies or other tracking techniques, are documented and described in the privacy notice.
Use Case(s)	The entity's privacy notice discloses the types of personal information collected, the sources and methods used to collect personal information, and whether information is developed or acquired about individuals, such as buying patterns. Types of personal information collected include the following: ■ Financial (for example, financial account information) ■ Health (for example, information about physical or mental status or history) ■ Demographic (for example, age, income range, social geocodes) Methods of collecting and third-party sources of personal information include the following: ■ Credit reporting agencies ■ Over the telephone ■ Via the Internet using forms, cookies, or Web beacons The entity's privacy notice discloses whether it uses cookies and Web beacons and how they are used. The notice also describes the consequences if the cookie is refused.
Rationale	The fourth principle of the Generally Accepted Privacy Principles (GAPP) is Collection. This principle requires that the entity collect personal information only for the purposes identified in the notice.
Priority	Critical/**High**/Medium/Low
Constraints	NA
Comments	NA

Table 4.82 describes the requirement for the use of personal information.

Table 4.82   Use of Personal Information

Req. ID: SR-PRIV-009	Category: SECURITY
Subcategory(ies)/Tags	Privacy, Use
Name	Use of Personal Information
Requirement	Personal information is used only for the purposes identified in the notice and only if the individual has provided implicit or explicit consent, unless a law or regulation specifically requires otherwise.
Use Case(s)	Systems and procedures are in place to ensure that personal information is used: ■ In conformity with the purposes identified in the entity's privacy notice ■ In agreement with the consent received from the individual ■ In compliance with applicable laws and regulations
Rationale	The fifth principle of the Generally Accepted Privacy Principles (GAPP) is Use and Retention. This principle requires that the entity limit the use of personal information to the purpose identified in the notice and for which the individual has provided implicit or explicit consent.
Priority	Critical/**High**/Medium/Low
Constraints	NA
Comments	Some regulations have specific provisions concerning the use of personal information. Examples are the GLBA, the Health Insurance Portability and Accountability Act (HIPAA), and the Children's Online Privacy Protection Act (COPPA).

Table 4.83 describes the requirement for retention of private information.

Table 4.83   Retention of Personal Information

Req. ID: SR-PRIV-010	Category: SECURITY
Subcategory(ies)/Tags	Privacy, Retention
Name	Retention of Personal Information
Requirement	Personal information is retained for no longer than necessary to fulfill the stated purposes, unless a law or regulation specifically requires otherwise.
Use Case(s)	The entity: ■ Documents its retention policies and disposal procedures ■ Retains, stores, and disposes of archived and backup copies of records in accordance with its retention policies ■ Ensures personal information is not kept beyond the standard retention time unless a justified business or legal reason for doing so exists
Rationale	The fifth principle of the Generally Accepted Privacy Principles (GAPP) is Use and Retention. This principle requires that the entity limit the use of personal information to the purpose identified in the notice and for which the individual has provided implicit or explicit consent.
Priority	Critical/**High**/Medium/Low
Constraints	NA
Comments	Some laws specify the retention period for personal information. For example, HIPAA has retention requirements on accounting for disclosures of personal health information—three years for electronic health records and six years for nonelectronic health records. Other statutory record retention requirements may exist; for example, certain data may need to be retained for tax purposes or in accordance with employment laws.

Table 4.84 describes the requirement for disposal, destruction, and redaction of personal information.

Table 4.84   Disposal, Destruction, and Redaction of Personal Information

Req. ID: SR-PRIV-011	Category: SECURITY
Subcategory(ies)/Tags	Privacy, Disposal, Destruction, Redaction
Name	Disposal, Destruction, and Redaction of Personal Information
Requirement	Personal information no longer retained is anonymized, disposed of, or destroyed in a manner that prevents loss, theft, misuse, or unauthorized access.
Use Case(s)	The entity: ■ Erases or destroys records in accordance with the retention policies, regardless of the method of storage (for example, electronic, optical media, or paper based) ■ Disposes of original, archived, backup and ad hoc or personal copies of records in accordance with its destruction policies ■ Documents the disposal of personal information ■ Within the limits of technology, locates and removes or redacts specified personal information about an individual as required—for example, removing credit card numbers after the transaction is complete ■ Regularly and systematically destroys, erases, or makes anonymous personal information no longer required to fulfill the identified purposes or as required by laws and regulations
Rationale	The fifth principle of the Generally Accepted Privacy Principles (GAPP) is Use and Retention. This principle requires that the entity limit the use of personal information to the purpose identified in the notice and for which the individual has provided implicit or explicit consent.
Priority	Critical/**High**/Medium/Low

Table 4.84 Disposal, Destruction, and Redaction of Personal Information

Constraints	NA
Comments	Consideration should be given to using the services of companies that provide secure destruction services for personal information. Certain of these companies will provide a certificate of destruction where needed.
	Certain archiving techniques, such as DVDs, CDs, microfilm, or microfiche may not permit the removal of individual records without destruction of the entire database contained on such media.

Table 4.85 describes the requirement for access by individuals to their personal information.

Table 4.85 Access by Individuals to Their Personal Information

Req. ID: SR-PRIV-012	Category: SECURITY
Subcategory(ies)/Tags	Privacy, Access
Name	Access by Individuals to Their Personal Information
Requirement	Individuals are able to determine whether the entity maintains personal information about them and, upon request, may obtain access to their personal information.
Use Case(s)	Procedures are in place to: ■ Determine whether the entity holds or controls personal information about an individual ■ Communicate the steps to be taken to gain access to the personal information ■ Respond to an individual's request on a timely basis ■ Provide a copy of personal information, upon request, in printed or electronic form that is convenient to both the individual and the entity ■ Record requests for access and actions taken, including denial of access and unresolved complaints and disputes

Table 4.85   Access by Individuals to Their Personal Information

Rationale	The sixth principle of the Generally Accepted Privacy Principles (GAPP) is Access. This principle requires that the entity provide individuals with access to their personal information for review and update.
Priority	Critical/**High**/Medium/Low
Constraints	NA
Comments	

Table 4.86 describes the requirement for access by individuals to their personal information.

Table 4.86   Updating or Correcting Personal Information

Req. ID: SR-PRIV-013	Category: SECURITY
Subcategory(ies)/Tags	Privacy, Access
Name	Updating or Correcting Personal Information
Requirement	Individuals are able to update or correct personal information held by the entity. If practical and economically feasible to do so, the entity provides such updated or corrected information to third parties that previously were provided with the individual's personal information.
Use Case(s)	The entity: ■ Describes the process an individual must follow to update or correct personal information records (for example, in writing, by phone, by e-mail, or by using the entity's Web site) ■ Verifies the accuracy and completeness of personal information that an individual updates or changes (for example, by edit and validation controls, and forced completion of mandatory fields) ■ Records the date, time, and identification of the person making the change if the entity's employee is making a change on behalf of an individual

Table 4.86   Updating or Correcting Personal Information

Use Case(s)	▪ Notifies third parties to whom personal information has been disclosed of amendments, erasures, or blocking of personal information, if it is possible and reasonable to do so
Rationale	The sixth principle of the Generally Accepted Privacy Principles (GAPP) is Access. This principle requires that the entity provide individuals with access to their personal information for review and update.
Priority	Critical/**High**/Medium/Low
Constraints	NA
Comments	NA

Table 4.87 describes the requirement for disclosure of personal information.

Table 4.87   Disclosure of Personal Information

Req. ID: SR-PRIV-014	Category: SECURITY
Subcategory(ies)/Tags	Privacy, Disclosure
Name	Disclosure of Personal Information
Requirement	Personal information is disclosed to third parties only for the purposes described in the notice, and for which the individual has provided implicit or explicit consent, unless a law or regulation specifically requires or allows otherwise.
Use Case(s)	Systems and procedures are in place to: ▪ Prevent the disclosure of personal information to third parties unless an individual has given implicit or explicit consent for the disclosure Document the nature and extent of personal information disclosed to third parties

Table 4.87   Disclosure of Personal Information

Use Case(s)	■ Test whether disclosure to third parties is in compliance with the entity's privacy policies and procedures, or as specifically allowed or required by law or regulation ■ Document any third-party disclosures for legal reasons
Rationale	The seventh principle of the Generally Accepted Privacy Principles (GAPP) is Disclosure to Third Parties. This principle requires that the entity disclose personal information to third parties only for the purposes identified in the notice and only with the implicit or explicit consent of the individual.
Priority	Critical/**High**/Medium/Low
Constraints	NA
Comments	Personal information may be disclosed through various legal processes to law enforcement or regulatory agencies. Some laws and regulations have specific provisions for the disclosure of personal information. Some permit disclosure of personal information without consent whereas others require verifiable consent.

Table 4.88 describes the requirement for protection of personal information from third parties.

Table 4.88   Protection of Personal Information

Req. ID: SR-PRIV-015	Category: SECURITY
Subcategory(ies)/Tags	Privacy, Disclosure
Name	Protection of Personal Information

Table 4.88   Protection of Personal Information (continued)

Requirement	Personal information is disclosed only to third parties who have agreements with the entity to protect personal information in a manner consistent with the relevant aspects of the entity's privacy policies or other specific instructions or requirements. The entity has procedures in place to evaluate that the third parties have effective controls to meet the terms of the agreement, instructions, or requirements.
Use Case(s)	When providing personal information to third parties, the entity enters into contracts that require a level of protection of personal information equivalent to that of the entity's. In doing so, the entity:

When providing personal information to third parties, the entity enters into contracts that require a level of protection of personal information equivalent to that of the entity's. In doing so, the entity:

- Limits the third party's use of personal information to purposes necessary to fulfill the contract
- Communicates the individual's preferences to the third party
- Refers any requests for access or complaints about the personal information transferred by the entity to a designated privacy executive, such as a corporate privacy officer
- Specifies how and when third parties are to dispose of or return any personal information provided by the entity

The entity evaluates compliance with such contract using one or more of the following approaches to obtain an increasing level of assurance depending on its risk assessment:

- The third party responds to a questionnaire about their practices.
- The third party self-certifies that its practices meet the entity's requirements based on internal audit reports or other procedures.
- The entity performs an onsite evaluation of the third party.

The entity receives an audit or similar report provided by an independent auditor.

Table 4.88   Protection of Personal Information (continued)

Rationale	The seventh principle of the Generally Accepted Privacy Principles (GAPP) is Disclosure to Third Parties. This principle requires that the entity disclose personal information to third parties only for the purposes identified in the notice and only with the implicit or explicit consent of the individual.
Priority	Critical/**High**/Medium/Low
Constraints	NA
Comments	The entity is responsible for personal information in its possession or custody, including information that has been transferred to a third party.
	Some regulations (for example, from the U.S. federal financial regulatory agencies) require that an entity take reasonable steps to oversee appropriate service providers by exercising appropriate due diligence in the selection of service providers.
	Some jurisdictions, including some countries in Europe, require entities that transfer personal information to register with their regulatory body prior to transfer.
	PIPEDA requires a comparable level of protection while the personal information is being processed by a third party.
	Article 25 of the EU's Directive requires that such transfers take place only where the third party ensures an adequate level of protection.

Table 4.89 describes the requirement for logical access controls.

Table 4.89   Logical Access Controls

Req. ID: SR-PRIV-016	Category: SECURITY
Subcategory(ies)/Tags	Privacy, Security for Privacy
Name	Logical Access Controls

Table 4.89   Logical Access Controls (continued)

Requirement	Logical access to personal information is restricted by procedures that address the following matters:
	■ Authorizing and registering internal personnel and individuals
	■ Identifying and authenticating internal personnel and individuals
	■ Making changes and updating access profiles
	■ Granting privileges and permissions for access to IT infrastructure components and personal information
	■ Preventing individuals from accessing anything other than their own personal or sensitive information
	■ Limiting access to personal information to only authorized internal personnel based upon their assigned roles and responsibilities
	■ Distributing output only to authorized internal personnel
	■ Restricting logical access to offline storage, backup data, systems, and media
	■ Restricting access to system configurations, super-user functionality, master passwords, powerful utilities, and security devices (for example, firewalls)
	■ Preventing the introduction of viruses, malicious code, and unauthorized software
Use Case(s)	NA
Rationale	The eighth principle of the Generally Accepted Privacy Principles (GAPP) is Security for Privacy. This principle requires that the entity protect personal information against unauthorized access (both physical and logical).
Priority	Critical/**High**/Medium/Low
Constraints	NA
Comments	NA

Table 4.90 describes the requirement for physical access controls.

Table 4.90   Physical Access Controls

Req. ID: SR-PRIV-017	Category: SECURITY
Subcategory(ies)/Tags	Privacy, Security for Privacy
Name	Physical Access Controls
Requirement	Physical access is restricted to personal information in any form (including the components of the entity's system(s) that contain or protect personal information). Systems and procedures are in place to: ■ Manage logical and physical access to personal information, including hard copy, archival, and backup copies ■ Log and monitor access to personal information ■ Prevent the unauthorized or accidental destruction or loss of personal information ■ Investigate breaches and attempts to gain unauthorized access ■ Communicate investigation results to the appropriate designated privacy executive ■ Maintain physical control over the distribution of reports containing personal information ■ Securely dispose of waste containing confidential information (for example, shredding)
Use Case(s)	NA
Rationale	The eighth principle of the Generally Accepted Privacy Principles (GAPP) is Security for Privacy. This principle requires that the entity protect personal information against unauthorized access (both physical and logical).
Priority	Critical/**High**/Medium/Low
Constraints	NA
Comments	NA

Table 4.91 describes the requirement for accuracy and completeness of personal information.

Table 4.91 Accuracy and Completeness of Personal Information

Req. ID: SR-PRIV-018	Category: SECURITY
Subcategory(ies)/Tags	Privacy, Quality of Personal Information
Name	Accuracy and Completeness of Personal Information
Requirement	Personal information is accurate and complete for the purposes for which it is to be used. Systems and procedures are in place to:
	■ Edit and validate personal information as it is collected, created, maintained, and updated
	■ Record the date when the personal information is obtained or updated
	■ Specify when the personal information is no longer valid
	■ Specify when and how the personal information is to be updated and the source for the update (for example, annual reconfirmation of information held and methods for individuals to proactively update personal information)
	■ Indicate how to verify the accuracy and completeness of personal information obtained directly from an individual, received from a third party (see 4.2.3, "Collection From Third Parties"), or disclosed to a third party (see 7.2.2, "Protection of Personal Information")
	■ Ensure personal information used on an ongoing basis is sufficiently accurate and complete to make decisions, unless clear limits exist for the need for accuracy

Table 4.91   Accuracy and Completeness of Personal Information (continued)

Requirement	■ Ensure personal information is not routinely updated unless such a process is necessary to fulfill the purposes for which it is to be used The entity undertakes periodic assessments to check the accuracy of personal information records and to correct them, as necessary, to fulfill the stated purpose.
Use Case(s)	
Rationale	The ninth principle of the Generally Accepted Privacy Principles (GAPP) is Quality. This principle requires that the entity maintain accurate, complete, and relevant personal information for the purposes identified in the notice.
Priority	Critical/**High**/Medium/Low
Constraints	NA
Comments	NA

Table 4.92 describes the requirement for inquiry, complaint, and dispute process.

Table 4.92   Inquiry, Complaint, and Dispute Process

Req. ID: SR-PRIV-019	Category: SECURITY
Subcategory(ies)/Tags	Privacy, Monitoring and Enforcement
Name	Inquiry, Complaint, and Dispute Process
Requirement	A process is in place to address inquiries, complaints, and disputes. The corporate privacy officer or other designated individual is authorized to address privacy related complaints, disputes, and other problems. Systems and procedures are in place that allow for: ■ Procedures to be followed in communicating and resolving complaints about the entity

Table 4.92   Inquiry, Complaint, and Dispute Process (continued)

Requirement	■ Action that will be taken with respect to the disputed information until the complaint is satisfactorily resolved ■ Remedies to be available in case of a breach of personal information, and how to communicate this information to an individual ■ Recourse and a formal escalation process to be in place to review and approve any recourse offered to individuals Contact information and procedures to be followed with any designated third-party dispute resolution or similar service (if offered)
Use Case(s)	NA
Rationale	The tenth principle of the Generally Accepted Privacy Principles (GAPP) is Monitoring and Enforcement. This principle requires that the entity monitor compliance with its privacy policies and procedures and have procedures to address privacy-related inquiries and disputes.
Priority	Critical/**High**/Medium/Low
Constraints	NA
Comments	NA

Table 4.93 describes the requirement for ongoing monitoring of controls.

Table 4.93   Ongoing Monitoring

Req. ID: SR-PRIV-020	Category: SECURITY
Subcategory(ies)/Tags	Privacy, Monitoring and Enforcement
Name	Ongoing Monitoring

Table 4.93   Ongoing Monitoring

Requirement	Ongoing procedures are performed for monitoring the effectiveness of controls over personal information, based on a risk assessment, and for taking timely corrective actions where necessary. Ongoing procedures are performed to monitor the effectiveness of controls over personal information, based on a risk assessment, and to take timely corrective actions where necessary. The entity uses the following: ■ Control reports ■ Trend analysis ■ Training attendance and evaluations ■ Complaint resolutions ■ Regular internal reviews ■ Internal audit reports ■ Independent audit reports covering controls at service organizations ■ Other evidence of control effectiveness The selection of controls to be monitored and the frequency with which they are monitored are based on the sensitivity of the information and the risks of possible exposure of the information.
Use Case(s)	Examples of such controls are as follows: ■ Policies require that all employees take initial privacy training within 30 days of employment. Ongoing monitoring activities would include a review of selected employees' human resource files to determine whether they contain the appropriate evidence of course completion.

Table 4.93   Ongoing Monitoring

Use Case(s)	<ul><li>Policies require that whenever an employee changes job responsibilities or is terminated, such employee's access to personal information be reviewed and appropriately modified or terminated within 24 hours (or immediately in the case of employee termination). This is controlled by an automated process within the human resource system, which produces a report of employee status changes that requires supervisor action to avoid automatic termination of access. This is monitored by the security group, which receives copies of these reports and the related supervisor actions.</li><li>Policies state that confirmation of a privacy-related complaint is provided to the complainant within 72 hours, and if not resolved within 10 working days, then the issue is escalated to the CPO. The control is a log used to record privacy complaints, including complaint date, and subsequent activities through to resolution. The monitoring activity is the monthly review of such logs for consistency with this policy.</li></ul>
Rationale	The tenth principle of the Generally Accepted Privacy Principles (GAPP) is Monitoring and Enforcement. This principle requires that the entity monitor compliance with its privacy policies and procedures and have procedures to address privacy-related inquiries and disputes.
Priority	Critical/**High**/Medium/Low
Constraints	NA
Comments	NA

4.16   Summary

Chapter 4 contains 93 software security requirements intended for you to reuse and customize as you prepare system specification documents for each application you're planning on developing.

In Chapter 5, you'll find another set of security-related requirements intended for the application operating environment and the deployment of infrastructure that contributes to the operating environment.

4.17   References

1. "Common Criteria Part 2: Security Functional Requirements," The Common Criteria Portal, accessed February 26, 2011, www.commoncriteriaportal.org/cc.

2. "Introducing Generally Accepted Privacy Principles," American Insitute of CPAs, accessed April 30, 2011, www.aicpa.org/InterestAreas/InformationTechnology/Resources/ Privacy/GenerallyAcceptedPrivacyPrinciples/Pages/default.aspx.

3. "Security Criteria," BITS/Financial Services Roundtable, accessed February 26, 2011, www.bitsinfo.org/ c_security_criteria.html.

4. Firesmith, D. G., *Engineering Security Requirements*, accessed January 3, 2011, www.jot.fm/issues/issue_2003_01/column6.

Chapter 5

Security Services for the Application Operating Environment

In Chapter 4, we covered detailed standalone requirements for the security features and controls that are contained directly within application software itself. Some of these features require the application to invoke services that should be provided by the application runtime environment (like logging).

In Chapter 5, we'll take a look at the security services that are best *pushed down* into the operating environment and published to developers with open interfaces that are used to gain access to the service. Services, in this sense, are meant as functions needed by application software to perform security work but should *not* be created by business systems developers.

By implementing security functions as infrastructure services, organizations are better served for a variety of reasons:

- Standardized functions that are made available to all developers offer a more maintainable, robust, and resilient set of processes that can be centrally managed by those in the best position to develop, procure, or offer security services that are reusable, repeatable, and reliable.
- Developers are left to concentrate on business function development without needing to be expert in the development of utilities and services for enterprise use.
- Pushing Policy Enforcement Points (PEPs) into the infrastructure makes it much more difficult to bypass them or subvert their execution.
- Centralized monitoring and reporting, in a consistent and repeatable fashion, offers management a more holistic view of operations as they're happening in real time.

- Auditing security functions is made simpler and yields a better picture of what's actually happening across multiple applications and systems.
- Vulnerabilities discovered in centralized security services can be isolated and eliminated or countered for all applications that depend on these services.
- Software and infrastructure can be swapped out for new or improved applications and tools and, as long as their interfaces don't change, applications using those components are insulated from those changes or updates if the APIs to invoke those services don't also change.

To explore what these infrastructure security services should do, we'll take a look at The Open Group Architecture Framework (TOGAF) as a useful model.

5.1   The Open Group Architecture Framework (TOGAF)

The Open Group Architecture Framework, or TOGAF, is:

> . . . a framework—a detailed method and a set of supporting tools—for developing an enterprise architecture. TOGAF may be used freely by any organization wishing to develop their own enterprise architecture . .
>
> TOGAF was developed by members of The Open Group, working within the Architecture Forum (www.opengroup.org/architecture). The original development of TOGAF Version 1 in 1995 was based on the Technical Architecture Framework for Information Management (TAFIM) by the U.S. Department of Defense (DoD). The DoD gave The Open Group permission and encouragement to create TOGAF by building on the TAFIM.[1]

An architecture framework is a tool used for developing a broad range of different architectures. Frameworks both describe a method for designing an information system as sets of building blocks and show how those building blocks fit and work together.

In the information security realm, TOGAF describes a Technical Reference Model (TRM) that provides both an abstract model and taxonomy for infrastructure services.

Adopters of TOGAF view infrastructure as a series of "services" to applications and other infrastructure elements. By treating controls and features as infrastructure services, you help to meet the principles of keeping the development of security controls out of the hands of business systems developers, and encourage the use of infrastructure-enabled security that developers simply invoke as needed in their applications. Furthermore, by pushing common security services into the infrastructure, you can better manage their development, testing, and rollout, knowing that they are created with the highest quality and used in the most efficient ways.

The U.S. government and many of the states have adopted some form of TOGAF for their own enterprise architecture implementation. There are a number of publically available sites on the Internet to view how the federal and state governments have taken it upon themselves to implement a TRM. As one example, the State of Illinois operates[2] an *Enterprise Architecture and Taxonomy Database* for users of state IT services to locate business applications, standardized products, reporting, and online help.

5.2   Standardizing Tools for an Enterprise Architecture

When establishing common services as infrastructure-enabled services, it's vital to maintain some semblance of control over the proliferation and implementation of commercial-off-the-shelf (COTS) applications and systems throughout the production environment. Business development teams *love* to bring in new systems for their own selfish uses without actually understanding the implications and costs of operations support.

Sometimes, these applications perform their own security functions, which violates centralizing security services to infrastructure PEPs. A better bet is to standardize on infrastructure COTS or in-house solutions and stop the procurement and implementation of one-off or corner-case applications.

Through standardization, you can implement best-of-breed or best-in-class COTS tools, provided that you offer developers an interface layer (APIs or middleware) that rarely changes and insulates developers from any changes as infrastructure tools change and improve. As you'll see in various sections of the TRM described below, standardization includes common services like directory services, single-sign-on (SSO), hardware-based cryptographic support and key management, monitoring and logging systems, and the like.

5.3   Security Technical Reference Model (TRM)

Security services[3] are necessary to protect sensitive information in the information system. The appropriate level of protection is determined based upon the value of the information to the business area end users and the perception of threats to it.

To be effective, security needs to be made strong, must never be taken for granted, and must be designed into an architecture and not bolted on afterwards. Whether a system is stand-alone or distributed, security must be applied to the whole system. It must not be forgotten that the requirement for security extends not only across the range of entities in a system but also through time.

In establishing a security architecture, the best approach is to consider what is being defended, what value it has, and what the threats to it are. The principal threats that should be countered are:

- Loss of confidentiality of data
- Unavailability of data or services
- Loss of integrity of data
- Unauthorized use of resources

These threats are countered through the following security services, described in the TOGAF Security Technical Reference Model:

- Identification and Authentication services
- System Entry Control services
- Audit services
- Access Control services
- Nonrepudiation services
- Security Management services
- Trusted Recovery services
- Encryption services
- Trusted Communication services

Think of the Security TRM as an *abstraction of the services* that application software needs to operate within a specific infrastructure. By looking at the requirements as a series of necessary services, you can quickly identify the most effective PEPs within the infrastructure and plan on meeting those needs using a baked-in set of services that anyone—with the proper authority—can use for requesting access to protected resources.

We'll examine each of the TRM areas in the following sections.

5.3.1   Identification and Authentication

Identification and authentication (I&A) is needed to access protected resources, typically using IDs and passwords. A user ID is offered by a human (or other computer program) to an application to *identify* itself. The password is used to *authenticate* the ID. I&A enables a user to state, for example, "I'm John T. Smith, and I can prove it." The ID identifies and the password authenticates. This is why protecting passwords is critical to the success of any I&A process.

Identification and Authentication services provide:

- Identification, accountability, and audit of users and their actions
- Authentication and account data
- Protection of authentication data
- Active user status information
- Password authentication and password expiry and reset mechanisms

A good example of an I&A system is an *identity management system* (like LDAP or other commercial identity manager software) for the enterprise. By using a centralized identity manager, developers are freed from the burden of creating their own mechanisms, and users benefit by requiring fewer IDs and passwords they'll need to remember. Password expiration is better controlled as well, since a single PEP will ensure that passwords are changed regularly. Identity management systems also help with deprovisioning or restricting the use of an ID, in the case of people leaving the company, leaving a role, or violating policies. Furthermore, by limiting the number of IDs and passwords in the environment, fewer user information stores help to improve information management of users, their related attributes, and the activities they perform while logged in.

5.3.2   System Entry Control

System entry control services[4] provide:

- Warning to unauthorized users that the system is security-aware
- Authentication of users

- Information, displayed on entry, about previous successful and unsuccessful login attempts
- User-initiated locking of a session, preventing further access until the user has been reauthenticated

Services in this area are responsible for displaying banners that warn would-be users that the system is being monitored and force them to agree to the terms and conditions for using the system. It also includes services that tell a user when authentication fails, but does not tell them where it failed or how, thus reducing information leakage and improper error handling (two key security vulnerabilities that lead to security incidents). The service might also let the user know about successful and unsuccessful log-on attempts, and allows the user to "lock" their interactive session with a system until they reauthenticate (think password-protected screen savers).

5.3.3 Audit

Audit services provide:

- Authorized control and protection of the audit trail
- Recording (logging) of detailed information security-relevant events
- Audit trail control, management, and inspection

Centralizing audit services is *one of the best choices* you can make in infrastructure planning. Logging and audit are two favorite targets of hackers to use when carrying out an attack. If it's possible to disable logging, hackers will first disable it, perform their criminal acts, and reenable it, making it impossible to determine what happened, where, when, and by whom.

In creating an enterprise audit and logging service, you can direct all application and system event- and security-logging activities to a specific internal system that will protect the integrity of audit data, control who has access to audit data, reduce the chances of log files filling up and stopping applications, and help IT management view what's going on within the enterprise from end-to-end, as well as within specific applications or operating or network platforms.

5.3.4   Access Control

Access Control services provide:

- Access control attributes for subjects (such as people or processes) and objects (such as files)
- Enforcement of rules for assignment and modification of access control attributes
- Enforcement of access controls
- Control of object creation and deletion, including ensuring that reuse of objects does not allow subjects to accidentally gain access to information previously held in the object

While we looked at identification and authentication earlier, access control involves the next two phases of accessing resources: authorization and audit. Access control is needed to determine whether a specific user (subject) has the rights or permissions to gain access to a protected resource (object). This can be thought of as an implementation of "need to know." Just because a user has system access does not mean he or she has rights to access every resource within it. By centralizing access control, you can better manage your protected resources through an ability to examine who's trying to access what and what they do once access is granted. Access Control describes another series of PEP that must never be bypass-able and cannot be subverted.

5.3.5   Nonrepudiation

Nonrepudiation services provide proof that a user carried out an action, or sent or received some information, at a particular time.

Nonrepudiation is necessary to *prove* that a person (or system) performed an action that they cannot deny having performed or participated in. Non-repudiation is often implemented using a public key infrastructure (PKI) that forces users (or other systems) to "sign" messages that constitute a transaction. A digital signature is an hash or message digest for a specific message that's encrypted with the sender's private key. The signature on the message is used to prove that ONLY the person holding the private key that's associated with the public key in their digital certificate could have signed that message. This all relies on the notion that a person's (or system's) private key is ALWAYS protected and never exposed, copied, or shared, with anyone else.

5.3.6 Security Management

Security management services provide:
- Secure system setup and initialization
- Control of security policy parameters
- Management of user registration data
- System resources and restrictions on the use of administrative functions

Security management services are needed to work hand-in-hand with I&A and access control services. These include services for managing the data associated with people who register for IDs and passwords (authenticating or personal data that can be checked prior to granting an ID), securing provisioning of new hardware and devices (standard, hardened operating systems images, etc.), controlling the access and changes of PEP policies, and allocating system resources to people and other applications. These are typically low-level functions that should be either well-controlled as human processes or technical implementations at the appropriate PEP for the specific service(s) requested.

5.3.7 Trusted Recovery

Trusted recovery services provide recovery facilities, such as restoring from backups in ways that do not compromise security protection.

Similar to audit services, trusted recovery helps via a centralized backup and restoration facility that simplifies and automates backup schedules for all critical and important resources and data. Rather than relying on each application or database to perform its own backups, centralized backup services can help ensure that the right data is backed up in the right way, at the right time, using the right media.

Trusted recovery is then used to restore operations to the most recent versions of software and data to assure continued operations in the event of a system or facility failure or disaster.

5.3.8 Encryption

Encryption services provide ways of encoding data such that it can only be read by someone who possesses an appropriate key or some other piece of secret information. In addition to providing data confidentiality for trusted communication, encryption services are often used in conjunction with other services, including I&A, system entry control, and access control services.

Encryption services, in this sense, can be thought of as an umbrella of services related to cryptography—both symmetric and asymmetric. These services may include the establishment, standardization, and management of services that application software might need for enforcing security policies (like encrypting sensitive or confidential data while at rest). You'll find PEPs wherever encryption is being used in the enterprise. Services in this family include standardized cryptosystems (e.g., AES, RSA, etc.), interfaces to invoke them, and the associated key management processes and tools that manage the expiry of keys, rekeying, and key compromise processes. Since good practices in key management are the foundation of effective cryptography, encryption services are needed to apply consistent rules, processes, and mechanisms to protect encryption keys from disclosure and misuse.

5.3.9   Trusted Communications

Trusted communications services provide:

- A secure way for communicating parties to authenticate themselves to each other without the risk of an eavesdropper subsequently masquerading as one of the parties
- A secure way of generating and verifying check values for data integrity
- Data encipherment and decipherment for confidentiality and other purposes
- A way to produce an irreversible hash of data for support of digital signature and nonrepudiation functions
- Generation, derivation, distribution, storage, retrieval, and deletion of cryptographic keys

Trusted communications services work hand-in-hand with encryption services to put to work the elements for effective and secure uses of cryptography. These services should *never* be left up to business applications developers to create or maintain—there are simply too many ways of introducing problems and errors into the system.

5.4   Summary

Security services are one category for which a wide view is essential—just like a chain is only as strong as its weakest link. Security is also one category of services for which the external environment has critical implications on the internal environment, since it's always a target for attack from both insiders and outsiders.

In Chapter 5, we looked at the TOGAF Security Technical Reference Model as an effective tool to abstract and describe the services needed by application software that is best implemented as infrastructure services. While we only scratched the surface of TOGAF and enterprise architecture in general, you can get a sense of where to draw the lines of what services should operate where and remove the responsibility for their implementation from business systems developers who are neither prepared nor qualified to develop them. By baking in security services, you do your developers a tremendous favor—you'll spare them the time and headaches of developing and operating enterprise-class services, but you'll also ease the efforts of developing software by doing the heavy-lifting for them through exposed services.

For more on TOGAF, visit the Open Group (www.opengroup.org).

In Chapter 6, we'll examine some ways of translating requirements into application and system designs to help simplify the work developers need to perform while enabling operations personnel and support personnel to take advantage of the features that makes software secure and resilient.

5.5   References

1.   "TOGAF Introduction," *Welcome to TOGAF—The Open Group Architecture Framework*, accessed April 11, 2011, http://pubs.opengroup.org/architecture/togaf8-doc/arch/chap01.html.

2.   "Enterprise Architecture and Taxonomy Database," State of Illinois Standards Site, accessed April 11, 2011, https://www.standards.illinois.gov/eatMain.asp.

3.   "Welcome to TOGAF® Version 9," Open Group Publications, accessed April 23, 2011, http://pubs.opengroup.org/architecture/togaf9-doc/arch.

4.   "Detailed Platform Taxonomy," TOGAF 8.1.1 Online, accessed April 23, 2011, http://pubs.opengroup.org/architecture/togaf8-doc/arch/chap20.html.

Chapter 6

Software Design Considerations for Security and Resilience

Over the last several chapters, we covered a wide variety of nonfunctional requirement specifications for security, quality, and resilience. We looked at the characteristics that make application software, systems of applications, and the runtime environment secure and resilient.

In this chapter, we'll move into the next layer of detail of design considerations for the application, application architecture, and the application operating environment to prepare you for turning requirements into actionable design steps. Here we'll cover design principles for secure and resilient applications and the infrastructure that supports software operations.

6.1 Design Issues

Figure 6.1, from Microsoft's *Security Engineering Explained: Patterns and Practices*,[1] points out some Web application design issues by overlaying them atop the typical three-tier Web architecture, consisting of Web server(s), application server(s), and database server(s).

Secure design practices are needed to address these issues and recommendations for addressing these issues are summarized in Table 6.1 below.

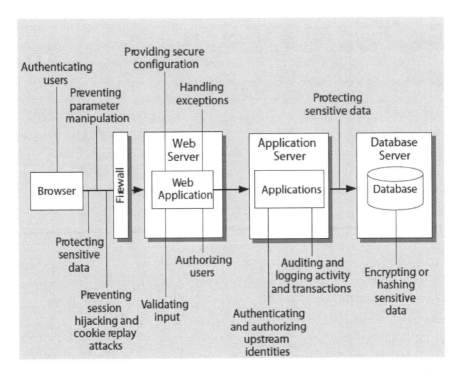

Figure 6.1   Source: Web Application Design Issues (Source: Security Engineering Explained," MSDN Patterns and Practices, Used with permission from Microsoft Corporation. Publication date: October 18, 2005)

As you'll see, some of these recommendations include taking advantage of infrastructure security services like those we discussed in Chapter 5.

Table 6.1   Recommendations for Addressing Web Application Design Issues

Input/Data Validation	Do not trust input; consider centralized input validation. Do not rely on client-side validation. Be careful with canonicalization issues. Constrain, reject, and sanitize input. Validate for type, length, format, and range.
Authentication	Use strong passwords. Support password expiration periods and account disablement. Do not store credentials (use one-way hashes with salt). Encrypt communication channels to protect authentication tokens. [AU: with salt? Do you mean "with a grain of salt" or is it just an IT term

Table 6.1   Recommendations for Addressing Web Application Design Issues

Authentication (cont)	I've missed?] It's an IT Security term. Basically a salt is a value that's used to create a message digest, along with other information, and the purpose is to foil a brute-force attack on passwords. Essentially, an attacker would need to know what the salt value is to append it to dictionary attack before it creates a hash (message digest) and then compares it to the stored password hashes.
Authorization	Use least privileged accounts. Consider authorization granularity. Enforce separation of privileges. Restrict user access to system level resources.
Configuration Management	Use least privileged process and service accounts. Do not store credentials in clear text. Use strong authentication and authorization on administration interfaces. Do not use the Local Security Authority (LSA). Secure the communication channel for remote administration.
Sensitive Data	Avoid storing secrets. Encrypt sensitive data over the wire.
Secured Communication Channel	Provide strong access controls for sensitive data stores.
Cryptography	Do not develop your own. Use proven and tested platform features. Keep unencrypted data close to the algorithm. Use the right algorithm and key size. Avoid custom key management approaches.
Periodic Cycling or Cryptographic Keys	Store keys in a restricted location.
Exception Management	Use structured exception handling. Never reveal sensitive application implementation details. Never log private data such as passwords. Consider a centralized exception management framework.

Table 6.1   Recommendations for Addressing Web Application Design Issues

Auditing and Logging	Identify malicious behavior. Know what good traffic looks like. Audit and log activity through all of the application tiers. Secure access to log files. Back up and regularly analyze log files.

Source: Design Guidelines for Secure Web Application, Chapter 4 (http://msdn.microsoft.com/en-us/library/ff648647.aspx)

6.2   Architecture and Design Considerations

A February 2011 *Software Assurance Pocket Guide*, "Architecture and Design Consideration for Secure Software,"[2] published by the Software Assurance Forum, offers a set of design principles that help organizations better design application software for security. These principles are summarized in Table 6.2 below.

Table 6.2   Design Principles for Secure Software

General Principle	Key Practices	Principle Design Conformance
Minimize the number of high-consequence targets	Principle of least privilege	Minimizes the number of actors in the system granted high levels of privilege and the amount of time any actor holds onto its privileges.
	Separation of privileges, duties, and roles	Ensures that no single entity (human or software) should have all the privileges required to modify, delete, or destroy the system, components and resources.
	Separation of domains	This practice makes separation of roles and privileges easier to implement.

Table 6.2   Design Principles for Secure Software (continued)

General Principle	Key Practices	Principle Design Conformance
Don't expose vulnerable or high-consequence components	Keep program data, executables, and configuration data separated	Reduces the likelihood that an attacker who gains access to program data will easily locate and gain access to program executables or control/configuration data.
	Segregate trusted entities from untrusted entities	Reduces the exposure of the software's high-consequence functions from its high-risk functions, which can be susceptible to attacks.
	Minimize the number of entry and exit points	Reduces the attack surface.
	Assume environment data is not trustworthy	Reduces the exposure of the software to potentially malicious execution environment components or attacker-intercepted and modified environment data.
	Use only trusted interfaces to environment resources	Reduces the exposure of the data passed between the software and its environment.

Table 6.2   Design Principles for Secure Software (continued)

General Principle	Key Practices	Principle Design Conformance
Deny attackers the means to compromise	Simplify the design	This practice minimizes the number of attacker-exploitable vulnerabilities and weaknesses in the system.
	Hold all actors accountable	This practice ensures that all attacker actions are observed and recorded, contributing to the ability to recognize and isolate/block the source of attack patterns.
	Timing, synchronization, and sequencing should be simplified to avoid issues	Modeling and documenting timing, synchronization, and sequencing issues will reduce the likelihood of race conditions, order dependencies, synchronization problems, and deadlocks.
	Make secure states easy to enter and vulnerable states difficult to enter	This practice reduces the likelihood that the software will be allowed to inadvertently enter a vulnerable state.
	Design for controllability	This practice makes it easier to detect attack paths and disengage the software from its interactions with attackers. Caution should be taken when using this approach, since it can open a whole range of new attack vectors.
	Design for secure failure	Reduces the likelihood that a failure in the software will leave it vulnerable to attack.

Source:Architecture and Design Considerations for Secure Software, Page 7-8 (https://buildsecurityin.us-cert.gov/swa/downloads/ Architecture_and_Design_Pocket_Guide_v1.3.pdf)

Some additional recommended design principles include:

- *Economy of mechanism*—Keep the design as simple and small as possible. Complexity is the enemy of security!
- *Fail-safe defaults*—Base access decisions on permission, rather than exclusion. This principle means that the default is lack of access, and the protection scheme identifies conditions under which access is permitted.
- *Complete mediation*—Every access to every object must be checked for authority. This principle, when systematically applied, is the primary underpinning of the protection system. It forces a system-wide view of access control, which in addition to normal operation includes initialization, recovery, shutdown, and maintenance.
- *Open design*—The design should not be secret. The mechanisms should not depend on the ignorance of potential attackers, but rather on the possession of specific, more easily protected, keys or passwords. In other words, avoid security through obscurity.
- *Separation of privilege*—A protection mechanism that requires two keys and two people (dual control and split knowledge) to unlock is more robust and flexible than one that allows access to the presenter with only a single key. Two keys apply to any situation in which two or more conditions must be met before access is granted.
- *Least privilege*—Every program and every user of the system should operate using the least set of privileges necessary to complete the job.
- *Least common mechanism*—Minimize the amount of mechanism common to more than one user and depended on by all users. Every shared mechanism represents a potential information path between users and must be designed with great care to be sure it does not unintentionally compromise security.
- *Psychological acceptability*—It is essential that the human interface be designed for ease of use, so that users routinely and automatically apply the protection mechanisms correctly.

6.3 Special Security Design Considerations for Payment Applications on Mobile Communications Devices

In April 2011, Visa Inc. issued Mobile Acceptance Best Practices[3] for those who develop or use payment applications that operate on mobile phones and other consumer mobile devices (like iPads and iPods). "Mobile devices that can facilitate acceptance of payments are an important advancement in payments that must balance the promise of an enhanced consumer and retailer shopping experience with enhanced security measures to protect sensitive cardholder information," said Eduardo Perez, head of global payment system risk, Visa, Inc.

Table 6.3   Visa's Mobile Acceptance Best Practices

Goal	Best Practice
Design and implement secure mobile payment acceptance solutions.	1. Provide payment acceptance applications and any associated updates in a secure manner with a known chain of trust. 2. Develop mobile payment acceptance applications based on secure coding guidelines. 3. Protect encryption keys that secure account data against disclosure and misuse in accordance with industry-accepted standards.
Ensure the secure use of mobile payment acceptance solutions.	1. Provide the ability to disable the mobile payment acceptance solution. 2. Provide functionality to track use and key activities within the mobile payment acceptance solution.

Table 6.3   Visa's Mobile Acceptance Best Practices

Limit exposure of account data that could be used to commit fraud.	1. Provide the ability to encrypt all public transmission of account data.
	2. Ensure that account data electronically read from a payment card is protected against fraudulent use by unauthorized applications in a consumer mobile device.
	3. Provide the ability to truncate or tokenize the Primary Account Number (PAN) after authorization to facilitate cardholder identification by the merchant.
	4. Protect stored PAN data and/or sensitive authentication data.

Source: "Visa Releases Mobile Acceptance Best Practices: http://corporate.visa.com/media-center/press-releases/press1121.jsp

You can find out more about Visa's Best Practices for Mobile Payment Acceptance at the Visa Inc. Cardholder Information Security Program[4] Web site.

6.4   Designing for Integrity

The U.S. Computer Emergency Readiness Team at US-CERT released Technical Information Paper (TIP-11-075-01), entitled *System Integrity Best Practices.*[5] The paper describes some design best practices to ensure software authenticity and user identities:

- Enable strong logging:
  - Enable logging for all centralized authentication services and collect the IP address of the system accessing the service, the username, the resource accessed, and whether the attempt was successful or not.
  - Limit the number of authentication attempts and lock out the user if the limit is reached. Security professionals should conduct a manual review before unlocking the account and prohibit automatic unlocks after a specified time period.
  - Conduct near-real-time log review for failed attempts per user and per unit of time, independent of successful logins, abnormal

successful logins, and lockouts. Correlate this data to identify anomalous activity.

- Limit remote access:
  - Restrict access by IP address wherever possible.
  - Limit concurrent logins to one per user.
- Apply additional defense-in-depth techniques:
  - Maximize complexity of passwords, passphrases, and personal identification numbers (PINs) whenever possible.
  - Enable defenses against key logging, such as forced frequent credential changing and updated antivirus (AV) signatures.
- Validate software:
  - Require validation of vendor-provided hash values or digital signatures prior to installation. If information is not customarily provided, request validation guidance from the vendor.
  - Exercise additional caution when receiving unsolicited or unexpected software media.
  - Establish installation baseline (e.g., file names, versions, hash values) and periodically revalidate this information.
  - Enable revocation checking to include Online Certificate Status Protocol (OCSP) and Certificate Revocation List (CRL) checking.

6.5 Architecture and Design Review Checklist

The Microsoft Developers Network (MSDN) Patterns and Practices Web site offers an Architecture and Design Review Checklist that you can use to help with design decisions. The checklist covers most software security, quality, and resilience characteristics within the architecture and design stages of the SDLC, including:

- Authentication
- Authorization
- Configuration management
- Sensitive data
- Session management
- Cryptography
- Parameter manipulation
- Exception management
- Auditing and logging[6]

Table 6.4   MSDN Architecture and Design Review Checklist

	YES	NO	N/A	Comments/Evidence/Rationale
Deployment and Infrastructure Considerations				
The design identifies, understands, and accommodates the company security policy.				
Restrictions imposed by infrastructure security (including available services, protocols, and firewall restrictions) are identified.				
The design recognizes and accommodates restrictions imposed by hosting environments (including application isolation requirements).				
The target environment code-access-security trust level is known.				
The design identifies the deployment infrastructure requirements and the deployment configuration of the application.				
Domain structures, remote application servers, and database servers are identified.				
The design identifies clustering requirements.				
The design identifies the application configuration maintenance points (such as what needs to be configured and what tools are available for an IDC admin).				
Secure communication features provided by the platform and the application are known.				

Table 6.4   MSDN Architecture and Design Review Checklist (continued)

	YES	NO	N/A	Comments/Evidence/Rationale
The design addresses Web farm considerations (including session state management, machine-specific encryption keys, Secure Sockets Layer [SSL], certificate deployment issues, and roaming profiles).				
The design identifies the certificate authority (CA) to be used by the site to support SSL.				
The design addresses the required scalability and performance criteria.				
Input Validation				
All entry points and trust boundaries are identified by the design.				
Input validation is applied whenever input is received from outside the current trust boundary.				
The design assumes that user input is malicious.				
Centralized input validation is used where appropriate.				
The input validation strategy that the application adopted is modular and consistent.				
The validation approach is to constrain, reject, and then sanitize input. Looking for known, valid, and safe input is much easier than looking for known malicious or dangerous input.				
Data is validated for type, length, format, and range.				

Table 6.4   MSDN Architecture and Design Review Checklist (continued)

	YES	NO	N/A	Comments/Evidence/Rationale
The design addresses potential canonicalization issues.				
Input file names and file paths are avoided where possible.				
The design addresses potential SQL injection issues.				
The design addresses potential cross-site scripting issues.				
The design does not rely on client-side validation.				
The design applies defense in depth to the input validation strategy by providing input validation across tiers.				
Output that contains input is encoded using HtmlEncode and UrltEncode.				
Authentication				
Application trust boundaries are identified by the design.				
The design identifies the identities that are used to access resources across the trust boundaries.				
The design partitions the Web site into public and restricted areas using separate folders.				
The design identifies service account requirements.				
The design identifies secure storage of credentials that are accepted from users.				

Table 6.4   MSDN Architecture and Design Review Checklist (continued)

	YES	NO	N/A	Comments/Evidence/Rationale
The design identifies the mechanisms to protect the credentials over the wire (SSL, IPSec, encryption and so on).				
Account management policies are taken into consideration by the design.				
The design ensures that minimum error information is returned in the event of authentication failure.				
The identity that is used to authenticate with the database is identified by the design.				
If SQL authentication is used, credentials are adequately secured over the wire (SSL or IPSec) and in storage (DPAPI).				
The design adopts a policy of using least-privileged accounts.				
Password digests (with salt) are stored in the user store for verification.				
Strong passwords are used.				
Authentication tickets (cookies) are not transmitted over nonencrypted connections.				
Authorization				
The role design offers sufficient separation of privileges (the design considers authorization granularity).				
Multiple gatekeepers are used for defense in depth.				

Table 6.4   MSDN Architecture and Design Review Checklist (continued)

	YES	NO	N/A	Comments/Evidence/Rationale
The application's login is restricted in the database to access-specific stored procedures.				
The application's login does not have permissions to access tables directly.				
Access to system level resources is restricted.				
The design identifies code access security requirements. Privileged resources and privileged operations are identified.				
All identities that are used by the application are identified and the resources accessed by each identity are known.				
Configuration Management				
Administration interfaces are secured (strong authentication and authorization is used).				
Remote administration channels are secured.				
Configuration stores are secured.				
Configuration secrets are not held in plain text in configuration files.				
Administrator privileges are separated based on roles (for example, site content developer or system administrator).				
Least-privileged process accounts and service accounts are used.				

Table 6.4   MSDN Architecture and Design Review Checklist (continued)

	YES	NO	N/A	Comments/Evidence/Rationale
Sensitive Data				
Secrets are not stored unless necessary. (Alternate methods have been explored at design time.)				
Secrets are not stored in code.				
Database connections, passwords, keys, or other secrets are not stored in plain text.				
The design identifies the methodology to store secrets securely. (Appropriate algorithms and key sizes are used for encryption. It is preferable that the Data Protection API (DPAPI) is used to store configuration data to avoid key management.)				
Sensitive data is not logged in clear text by the application.				
The design identifies protection mechanisms for sensitive data that is sent over the network.				
Sensitive data is not stored in persistent cookies.				
Sensitive data is not transmitted with the GET protocol.				
Session Management				
SSL is used to protect authentication cookies.				
The contents of authentication cookies are encrypted.				
Session lifetime is limited.				

Table 6.4   MSDN Architecture and Design Review Checklist (continued)

	YES	NO	N/A	Comments/Evidence/Rationale
Session state is protected from unauthorized access.				
Session identifiers are not passed in query strings.				
Cryptography				
Platform-level cryptography is used and it has no custom implementations.				
The design identifies the correct cryptographic algorithm (and key size) for the application's data encryption requirements.				
The methodology to secure the encryption keys is identified.				
The design identifies the key recycle policy for the application.				
Encryption keys are secured.				
DPAPI is used where possible to avoid key management issues.				
Keys are periodically recycled.				
Parameter Manipulation				
All input parameters are validated (including form fields, query strings, cookies, and HTTP headers).				
Cookies with sensitive data are encrypted.				
Sensitive data is not passed in query strings or form fields.				

Table 6.4   MSDN Architecture and Design Review Checklist (continued)

	YES	NO	N/A	Comments/Evidence/Rationale
HTTP header information is not relied on to make security decisions.				
View state is protected using MACs.				
Exception Management				
The design outlines a standardized approach to structured exception handling across the application.				
Application exception handling minimizes the information disclosure in case of an exception.				
The design identifies generic error messages that are returned to the client.				
Application errors are logged to the error log.				
Private data (for example, passwords) is not logged.				
Auditing and Logging				
The design identifies the level of auditing and logging necessary for the application and identifies the key parameters to be logged and audited.				
The design considers how to flow caller identity across multiple tiers (at the operating system or application level) for auditing.				
The design identifies the storage, security, and analysis of the application log files.				

Source: Microsoft.Developers Network (MSDN) Patterns and Practices Web site (http://msdn.microsoft.com/en-us/library/aa302332.aspx)

6.6   Summary

Chapter 6 covers a number of recommendations and tools to help you design applications and systems that meet nonfunctional requirements (NFRs) related to security and resilience. You saw how to address design issues as they relate to the multiple tiers of Web application deployments. You were also provided with a set of general principles that cover software architecture and design key practices. You saw some special design considerations for mobile payments, and finally, you were provided a useful checklist to use when conducting architecture and design analysis activities.

In Chapter 7, we'll show you how to use apply these principles and recommendations to convert NFRs into application and architectural designs that are testable, verifiable, and are proven to stand up to most malicious activity.

6.7   References

1. "Security Engineering Explained," MSDN Patterns and Practices Web site, accessed April 26, 2011, msdn.microsoft.com/en-us/library/ff648940.aspx.

2. "Architecture and Design Considerations for Secure Software," US-CERT Build Security In, accessed April 27, 2011, https://buildsecurityin.us-cert.gov/swa/downloads/Architecture_and_Design_Pocket_Guide_v1.3.pdf.

3. "Visa Releases Mobile Acceptance Best Practices," Visa Corporate Media Center, accessed April 28, 2011, http://corporate.visa.com/media-center/press-releases/press1121.jsp.

4. "Cardholder Information Security Program," Visa USA April 26, 2011,   http://usa.visa.com/merchants/risk_management/cisp.html.

5. "Technical Information Paper TIP-11-075-01 System Integrity best Practices," US-CERT, accessed May 3, 2011, www.us-cert.gov/reading_room/TIP11-075-01.pdf.

6. "Checklist: Architecture and Design Review," MSDN Patterns and Practices, accessed April 11, 2011, http://msdn.microsoft.com/en-us/library/aa302332.aspx.

Chapter 7

Best Practices for Converting Requirements to Secure Software Designs

At this point in the book, we've offered an in-depth look at security and resilience requirements for both application software and its operating environment. We have also looked some design considerations for building secure and high-quality software.

In Chapter 7, we'll focus on some of the best practices used to convert requirements into secure software designs.

7.1 Secure Design Approach

One way to convert all the security requirements into a secure design that is scalable for both small and large organizations is by reviewing existing requirements and their potential vulnerabilities and attacks and categorizing them into:

- Framework-level solutions
- Reusable APIs/libraries
- Code-level protection
- Perimeter-level protection

An example of how this works is shown in Table 7.1.

Table 7.1 Mapping vulnerabilities to design strategies

Vulnerabilities/ Threats	Framework	Reusable API/ Library	Perimeter	Code
Cross-Site Scripting	✕			

Table 7.1   Mapping vulnerabilities to design strategies (continued)

Cryptography		✕		
Denial of Service			✕	
Business Logic Bypass				✕

Perimeter-level solutions include network firewalls, application firewalls, load balancers, and other perimeter protection devices. Code-level protections are realized when developers fulfill the business security and quality requirements in source code. We'll describe what security frameworks and reusable security APIs/libraries are in the following sections.

7.2   Reusable Security APIs/Libraries

Application developers have no business writing security functions. Using security controls is different from building them. A better bet is to build and promulgate *standardized security APIs* for developers to reuse and integrate into their applications. These APIs perform vital security functions (input validation, encoding/decoding, cryptographic processing, user authentication, user authorization, error and event logging, error handling and so forth). The Open Web Application Security Project (OWASP) Enterprise Security API[1] is one such API that any organization can adopt and customize for its software development and operational processes. Developers will need education and training on using these security APIs and should be prevented from developing their own at all costs!

7.3   Security Frameworks

In addition to reusing security APIs in custom development work, security frameworks can help automatically prevent many well-known attacks, such as cross-site scripting, cross-site request forgery (CSRF), and others. These frameworks are built by a centralized application security development team under the guidance of a centralized application security management group and deployed to all production Web applications. These frameworks *automatically* provide security functions that counter well-known Web attacks.

Many existing frameworks, such as Spring and Struts, have *some* security features built in, but controls are frequently missing, incomplete, or wrong. After analyzing the gaps in each framework, some of the typical custom frameworks that can be built and deployed in any application infrastructure include: output encoding framework; input validation framework; and CSRF framework.

Where API calls need to be explicitly used by developers, these frameworks work invisibly and require no explicit action from the developers. For example, if developers fail to output encode the parameters sent to an HTML page, these frameworks will automatically do it for them.

7.4   Establishing and Following Best Practices for Design

Microsoft has done extensive work on secure design methodologies and considerations around security requirements and security recommendations and has described how these apply to Microsoft's own Security Development Lifecycle (SDL).[2]

The best time to influence a project's trustworthy design is early in its life cycle. Functional specifications may need to describe security features or privacy features that are directly exposed to users, such as requiring user authentication to access specific data or user consent before use of a high-risk privacy feature. Design specifications should describe how to implement these features and how to implement all functionality as secure features.

Secure features are defined as features with functionality that is well-engineered with regard to security, such as rigorously validating all data before processing it, or maintaining cryptographically strong APIs. Consider security and privacy concerns carefully and early when you design features, and avoid attempts to add or "bolt-on" security and privacy close to the end of a project's development.

7.5   Security Requirements

Following are some recommendations from Microsoft's SDL:

- Complete a security design review with a security advisor for any project or portion of a project that requires one. Some low-risk components might not require a detailed security design review.
- When developing with managed code, use strong-named assemblies and request minimal permission.
- For online services, all new releases must use the Relying Party Suite (RPS) v4.0 Software Development Kit (SDK). RPS provides

significant security advantages over the current Passport Manager (PPM) SDK, the most important being the elimination of the shared symmetric encryption keys, which mitigates security issues involving key distribution, deployment, and administration.

■ Comply with user account control (UAC) best practices to ensure that your application runs correctly as a nonadministrator. Exit criteria for this requirement is confirmation from the project team that it has analyzed and minimized the need for elevated privileges and followed best practices for operation in a UAC environment. Following this requirement enables teams to design and develop applications with a standard user in mind. This results in a reduced attack surface exposed by applications, thus increasing the security of the user and system.

■ If a program requires opening a port in the firewall, then the code that listens on the port for traffic must comply with certain documented quality requirements.

MSDN defines *managed code* as application software code written in one of the high-level programming languages that are available for use with the Microsoft .NET Framework:

All of these languages share a unified set of class libraries and can be encoded into an Intermediate Language (IL). A runtime-aware compiler compiles the IL into native executable code within a managed execution environment that ensures type safety, array bound and index checking, exception handling, and garbage collection.

By using managed code and compiling it in a managed execution environment, you can avoid many typical programming mistakes that lead to security holes and unstable applications. Also, many unproductive programming tasks are automatically taken care of, such as type safety checking, memory management, and destruction of unneeded objects.[3]

The result of using Managed Code is shorter development times and more secure and stable applications.

7.6   Security Recommendations

Microsoft's SDL Version 5.1 recommends the following activities in "Phase 2: Design" from the MSDN Library[2]:

- Include in all functional and design specifications a section that describes all impacts on security.
- Write a security architecture document that provides a description of a software project that focuses on security. Such a document should complement and reference existing traditional development collateral without replacing it. A security architecture document should contain, at a minimum:
- *Attack surface measurement.* After all design specifications are complete, define and document what the program's default and maximum attack surfaces are. The size of the attack surface indicates the likelihood of a successful attack. Therefore, your goal should be to minimize the attack surface. [. . .]
- *Product structure or layering.* Highly structured software with well-defined dependencies among components is less likely to be vulnerable than software with less structure. Ideally, software should be structured in a layered hierarchy so that higher components (layers) depend on lower ones. Lower layers should never depend on higher ones. Developing this sort of layered design is difficult and might not be feasible with legacy or preexisting software. However, teams that develop new software should consider layered and highly structured designs.

An application's attack surface is anywhere a user interacts with the application or anywhere the application interacts with other applications. These attack surface areas include user-supplied input fields, interfaces to other code (e.g. commercial off-the-shelf (COTS) APIs, open-source application code interfaces, etc.), and number of lines of code that increase the opportunities for programming errors.

7.7   What's an Attack Surface?

- Minimize default attack surface/enable least privilege.
- All feature specifications should consider whether the features should be enabled by default. If a feature is not used frequently, you should disable it. Consider carefully whether to enable by default those features that are used infrequently.
- If the program needs to create new user accounts, ensure that they have as little permission as possible for the required function and that they require strong passwords.

- Be very aware of access control issues. Always run code with the fewest possible permissions. When code fails, find out why it failed and fix the problem instead of increasing permissions. The more permissions any code has, the greater its exposure to abuse.
- *Default installations should be secure.* Carefully review for vulnerabilities all functionality and exposed features that are enabled by default and that constitute the attack surface.
- Consider a defense-in-depth approach. The most exposed entry points should have multiple protection mechanisms to reduce the likelihood of exploitation of any security vulnerabilities that might exist. If possible, review public sources of information for known vulnerabilities in competitive products, analyze them, and adjust your product's design accordingly.
- If the program is a new release of an existing product, examine past vulnerabilities in previous versions of the product and analyze their root causes. This analysis might uncover additional instances of the same classes of problems in the new release.
- Deprecate outdated functionality. If the product is a new release of an existing product, evaluate the support for older protocols, file formats, and standards, and strongly consider removing them in the new release. Older code written when security awareness was less prevalent almost always contains security vulnerabilities.
- Conduct a security review of all sample source code released with the product and use the same level of scrutiny as for object code released with the product.
- If the product is a new release of an existing product, consider migration of any possible legacy code from unmanaged code to managed code.
- Implement any new code using managed code whenever possible.
- When developing with managed code, take advantage of .NET security features:
- Refuse unneeded permissions.
- Request optional permissions.
- Use CodeAccessPermission Assert and LinkDemand carefully. Use Assert in as small a window as possible.
- Disable tracing and debugging before deploying ASP.NET applications.

7.8   What Is Managed Code?

- Watch for ambiguous representation issues. Hackers will try to force code to follow a dangerous path or URL by hiding their intent with escape characters or obscure conventions. Always design code to deal with full canonical representations, rather than acting on externally provided data. The canonical representation of something is the standard, most direct, and least ambiguous way to represent it.

- Remain informed about security issues in the industry. Attacks and threats evolve constantly, and staying current is important. Keep your team informed about new threats and vulnerabilities.

- Ensure that everyone on your team knows about unsafe functions and coding patterns. Maintain a list of your code's vulnerabilities. When you find new vulnerabilities, publish them. *Make security everyone's business.*

- Be careful with error messages. Sensitive information displayed in an error message can provide an attacker with privileged information, such as a file path on a server or the structure of a query. Such information makes it easier for an attacker to attack any defenses. In general, record detailed failure messages in a secure log, and give the user only enough information to describe what went wrong without technical details.

- For online services and/or line of business (LOB) applications, ensure the appropriate logging is enabled for forensics.

- For online services and/or LOB applications, make sure that page flow integrity checking is performed.

- Conduct a high-level security design review for hardware products that are new or being updated in the current release. The goal of a high-level hardware security design review is to identify aspects of the design that could lead to security vulnerabilities. This might include checks such as:
  - Methods of cryptographic key generation and storage.
  - Methods of data storage, including encryption. For example, does the design meet Microsoft Cryptographic Standards?
  - Methods of data manipulation.
  - The "business or customer impact" of the data being manipulated and stored. For example, whether the data could be considered High Business Impact (HBI), Moderate Business

Impact (MBI), or Low Business Impact (LBI) by the product's expected customers.

- Use of standard versus custom protocols.
- Presence of Joint Test Action Group (JTAG)/debugging back doors. JTAG is the common name used for the IEEE 1149.1 standard entitled Standard Test Access Port and Boundary-Scan Architecture for testing/debugging access ports using a boundary scan.
- Firmware upgrade features and procedures (security, process, and scalability).
- Firmware development process – /analyze, fuzzing and/or other security tools may be applicable.

- Implement an integration-points security design review. Enterprise server application suites, software-as-a-service (SaaS) offerings, and security products interact with a variety of other products and platforms in order to provide robust, enterprise-focused services. It is not sufficient to threat model these products by themselves because the points of interaction with other products are the source of many nuanced security issues. Conduct an integration-points security design review with dependent product teams across your end-to-end scenarios. Examples of products that should do this are:
  - Products designed to handle high business impact (HBI) data.
  - Enterprise applications and services.
  - Security products.
  - Software as a Service (SaaS)
  - The exit criteria for this recommendation is that the product teams and security reviewers/owners have reviewed and are satisfied with the security threat mitigations and validations provided at each point of integration.

- Implement strong log-out and session management. Proper session handling is one of the most important parts of Web application security. At the most fundamental level, sessions must be initiated, managed, and terminated in a secure manner. If a product employs an authenticated session, it must begin as an encrypted authentication event to avoid session fixation.
  - A session identifier/token must never be transmitted via the URL to avoid side-jacking via the referrer header or browser history.

- All session data must be maintained on the server, not the client, to avoid tampering.
- Sessions must be completely terminated on the server side via logout and timeout mechanisms. When multiple sessions are tied to a single authentication event, all of the sessions tied to that event must be terminated by logout/time-out.
- The following items must be met as part of the exit criteria for this recommendation:
  - When multiple sessions are tied to a single user identity, they must be collectively terminated on the server side at timeout or logout.
  - Authentication events must invalidate unauthenticated sessions and create a new session identifier.
  - Logout functionality is available on every page.
  - Session state, outside of a single identifier, is maintained on the server and not accepted from the user (including via cookie or header).
  - Session tokens are not present in the URI.
  - Timeout functionality is present and timeout thresholds are documented along with the rationale.

7.9   Understanding Business Requirements for Security Design

In addition to the generic security, quality, and resilience requirements, one of the critical inputs that significantly influence the design of application software are the business requirements. When analyzing and determining the security business requirements of the organization, you have to include these following factors, redacted from Tech FAQ.com:[4]

- *Business model*: The business model that the organization uses greatly influences the type of security an organization implements. An organization that has world-wide branches would have different security requirements from a business that has a single office.
- *Business processes*: To successfully implement security, you have to know how the business processes within the organization work. Be sure that security does not prevent business processes from being carried out efficiently or effectively.

- *Business growth*: As the business grows so too must the security policies and processes so that they are able to cater to growth.
- *Risk tolerance*: Determine the risk tolerance of the organization. The level of risk tolerance would differ between organizations for a variety of reasons. Make sure you have a consistent, repeatable, and understandable way of describing the balance between risk and reward.
- *Laws and regulations*: Determine whether there are any laws and regulations which with the organization must comply. This is especially important for security design work.
- *Existing security policies and procedures*: Determine what the current security policies and standards require of application software and development efforts.

7.10 Summary

In Chapter 7, you saw some of the best practices around converting requirements to secure designs and what Microsoft recommends for conducting a secure design phase of the SDLC.

In Chapter 8, you'll find test cases for the security requirements we covered throughout the book, and you'll discover a methodology to easily implement and integrate these test cases into your software test phase.

7.11 References

1. "Category: OWASP Enterprise Security API," OWASP, accessed April 3, 2011, http://www.owasp.org/index.php/Category:OWASP_Enterprise_ Security_API.

2. "SDL Phase 2: Design," MSDN Library, accessed April 9, 2011, http://msdn.microsoft.com/en-us/library/cc307414.aspx.

3. "What Is Managed Code?," MSDN Library, accessed April 11, 2011, http://msdn.microsoft.com/en-us/library/ms804960.aspx.

4. "Understanding Business Requirements for Security Design," NTech-FAQ, accessed April 10, 2011, http://www.tech-faq.com/understanding-business-requirements-for-security-design.html.

Chapter 8

Security Test Cases

In the last chapter, we looked at some of the best practices for converting security requirements into secure software designs. Chapter 8 details the test cases that correspond to each of the security requirements from Chapter 4. Each security requirement in Chapter 4 is tied to one or more test cases you'll find in this chapter. These test cases are meant for you to use when developing a *testing plan* sometime during the analysis phase of your project. This testing plan is then used for comprehensive testing of both the application's functional requirements and its security requirements.

8.1   Standardized Testing Policy

Chapter 8 introduces several principles and rationale for the testing for security requirements:

- Automated verification
- Manual verification
- Design verification
- Internal verification

These testing levels are described at length in Chapter 9. At this point in the book, it's important to understand the various testing approaches for applications.

Each application is different for several reasons–business requirements, programming language, the type of data it handles, platform, frameworks used, and so on. Based on the type of application some types of testing lend themselves to automation using both static and dynamic analysis tools.

Not all types of testing can be done using a single tool or even a single type of tool. For example, a static analysis tool can be efficient in finding issues such as infinite loops, buffer overflows, or even dead code, while a dynamic analysis tool might not be able to search for such issues. For a more detailed discussion on testing tools and methods, see Chapter 9.

8.2 Security Test Cases

In this section you'll find test cases organized into the same following categories as you saw in Chapter 4:

- Identification Requirements
- Authentication Requirements
- Authorization Requirements
- Security Auditing Requirements
- Confidentiality Requirements
- Integrity Requirements
- Availability Requirements
- Nonrepudiation Requirements
- Immunity Requirements
- Survivability Requirements
- Systems Maintenance Security Requirements

As mentioned earlier, these test cases directly tie back to the requirements specified in Chapter 4. These are provided to serve as a foundation or a starting point, and should not be considered a comprehensive list of all test cases. Depending on organizational requirements, you may prefer to add other test cases to this list or break down some test cases into multiple cases for tracking and validation purposes.

In the case of Privacy Requirements from Chapter 4 (SR-PRIV-001 through SR-PRIV-020), testing is not so clear cut. Many of the privacy controls that are not technical in nature are covered within other security controls, since the goals of protection are identical for security and privacy purposes. For nontechnical privacy controls, we recommend a detailed process-level audit, analysis review, and sign-off from the organization's privacy officer to ensure that all privacy related requirements are met in the application and the surrounding processes that rely on the application(s). Observation and other testing of functional requirements related to privacy protections will also help to reveal any issues with their implementation.

8.2.1   Test Cases for Identification Requirements

This section lists the test cases for the Identification requirements listed in chapter 4.

Table 8.1 documents the test case for Unique User IDs.

Table 8.1   Unique User IDs

Req. ID: STC-IDEN-001	Category: SECURITY
Subcategory(ies)/Tags	Identification, User ID, Login
Name	Unique User ID
Description	Verify that that no two entities in the software ecosystem carry that same internal or external identification.
Constraints	NA
Comments	This would involve verification of aliases, if any, and how those are mapped to actual users.

Tables 8.2.1 and 8.2.2 describe the test cases for ensuring that no backdoors exist in authentication systems.

Table 8.2.1   Preventing Backdoors in Authentication Systems

Req. ID: STC-IDEN-002-1	Category: SECURITY
Subcategory(ies)/Tags	Identification, User ID, Login, Backdoor
Name	Backdoor Prevention
Description	Verify that that all interfaces (regular application login, batch jobs, API calls, N/W interface) to the system mandate a valid user ID before allowing any access to the services.
Constraints	List of ALL available interfaces must be identified before this test can begin.
Comments	NA

Table 8.2.2   Preventing Backdoors in Authentication Systems

Req. ID: STC-IDEN-002-2	Category: SECURITY
Subcategory(ies)/Tags	Identification, User ID, Login, Backdoor
Name	Backdoor Prevention
Description	Verification that codebase (specifically the one involving authentication and authorization) using automated static analysis tools and manual security code review to ensure no such backdoor logic exists.
Constraints	One must understand that this test alone can never provide 100 percent assurance; hence, the organization would have to ensure that constant detection/monitoring is in place for critical software. A good reference on this matter is Ken Thompson's "Reflections on Trusting Trust."[1]
Comments	NA

Table 8.3 describes the test case for validating process identifier codes to establish accountability.

Table 8.3   Process Identifier Code

Req. ID: STC-IDEN-003	Category: SECURITY
Subcategory(ies)/Tags	Identification, User ID, Login, PID
Name	Process Identifier Code/Accountability
Description	Verify that that all system process (including but not limited to Process Spawning, Batch Jobs, etc.) associate the process with the corresponding user IDs of the user which invoked them.
Constraints	NA
Comments	Autonomous processes (such as print spooler) shall be associated with an identifier code, such as "system ownership."

Table 8.4 describes the test case for autodisabling user IDs.

Table 8.4   Autodisable User IDs

Req. ID: STC-IDEN-004	Category: SECURITY
Subcategory(ies)/Tags	Identification, User ID, Login, Backdoor
Name	Autodisable User IDs
Description	Verify that that system automatically disables an identifier if it remains inactive for a specified time period (configurable).
Constraints	NA
Comments	If the disabling process is not automatic, the tester must verify whether the system generates an autonomous message for the administrator indicating that a user ID has remained inactive for the specified period.

Table 8.5 describes the test case for maintaining security attributes.

Table 8.5   Security Attributes

Req. ID: STC-IDEN-005	Category: SECURITY
Subcategory(ies)/Tags	Identification, User ID, Security Metadata
Name	Security Attributes
Description	Verify that the application/system maintains the following list of security attributes for each user: user ID, group memberships, access control privileges, authentication information, and security-relevant roles.
Constraints	NA
Comments	NA

8.2.2   Test Cases for Authentication Requirements

This section lists the test cases for the authentication requirements listed in Chapter 5.

Table 8.6 describes the test case for credential security.

Table 8.6   Credential Security

Req. ID: STC-ATEN-001	Category: SECURITY
Subcategory(ies)/Tags	Authentication, Credentials, Passwords, Hashing
Name	Credential Security
Description	Verify that the passwords for all user accounts are stored in the database using a one way hash function.
Constraints	NA
Comments	Verify that each user ID has a unique salt for better security.

Table 8.7 describes the test case for replay attack protection.

Table 8.7   Replay Attack Protection

Req. ID: STC-ATEN-002	Category: SECURITY
Subcategory(ies)/Tags	Authentication, Credentials, Login, Replay Attack
Name	Replay Attack Protection
Description	Verify that time-bound passwords and biometric authentication credentials are being validated and rejected from being replayed to gain unauthorized access to the application.
Constraints	NA
Comments	The test must also validate that the transmission of these credentials are also protected in the first place.

Table 8.8 describes the test case for protecting against credential guessing to counter brute-force attacks on password systems.

Table 8.8   Protect Credential Guessing

Req. ID: STC-ATEN-003	Category: SECURITY
Subcategory(ies)/Tags	Authentication, Credential Enumeration, Login
Name	Protect Credential Guessing
Description	Verify that the application error messages do not reveal which part of the credential (user ID or password) is incorrect for a failed login attempt.
Constraints	This must be done for all possible types of logins allowed into the application.
Comments	Also verify whether brute-force detection and protection controls exist for the application.

Table 8.9 describes the test case for authenticating the server.

Table 8.9   Server Authentication

Req. ID: STC-ATEN-004	Category: SECURITY
Subcategory(ies)/Tags	Authentication, Credentials, Login
Name	Server Authentication
Description	Verify that the server is authenticating itself to the client by way of certificates (SSL, SSH, etc.) and the client can easily identify the server's authenticity.
Constraints	NA
Comments	At the very least, the portions of the application that handle sensitive information (like passwords, personal information, and financial information) shall do so with exceptions to other pages (https vs. http).

Table 8.10 describes the test case for reauthentication.

Table 8.10   Reauthentication

Req. ID: STC-ATEN-005	Category: SECURITY
Subcategory(ies)/Tags	Authentication, Credentials, Login
Name	Reauthentication
Description	For all state changing/critical transaction flows: Verify that the application forces the user to reauthenticate using the password or a second-level transaction password (or a one-time password if available).
Constraints	NA
Comments	Other risk management and fraud detection/prevention controls shall exist for the primary protection of the application data.

Table 8.11 describes the test case for protecting credentials.

Table 8.11   Protection of Credentials

Req. ID: STC-ATEN-006	Category: SECURITY
Subcategory(ies)/Tags	Authentication, Credentials, Login
Name	Protection of Credentials
Description	Verify that the passwords for all user accounts are never stored or transmitted in clear text. This shall include but not be limited to verifying databases, logfile, error messages, administrative console message, flat files on the application file systems, etc.
Constraints	NA
Comments	A security code review is suggested to confirm whether any occurrence of a clear text password, encryption key or other authentication information in the memory shall be overwritten immediately after use.

Table 8.12 describes the test case for password changes.

Table 8.12   Password Changes

Req. ID: STC-ATEN-007	Category: SECURITY
Subcategory(ies)/Tags	Authentication, Credentials, Login, Passwords
Name	Password Changes
Description	▪ Verify that the application forces a password change on the very first login for a user (specifically for auto-generated/administrated created passwords). ▪ The verifier shall try to forcefully navigate away from the password change page by using known URLs for the home page (or any other page) and confirm that the application does not allow such access. ▪ Verify that the application shall later on allow for regular password changes at user's will.
Constraints	NA
Comments	NA

Table 8.13 describes the test case for password aging.

Table 8.13   Password Aging

Req. ID: STC-ATEN-008	Category: SECURITY
Subcategory(ies)/Tags	Authentication, Credentials, Login, Passwords
Name	Password Aging
Description	▪ Verify that the passwords for all user accounts can be set to expire after a certain period of time. ▪ Verify that password actually expire after the set period and force the user to change the password.
Constraints	NA

Table 8.13   Password Aging (continued)

Comments	Verify that batch process and other systems that have a valid/approved business requirement not to have their password expire are not impacted by this feature.

Table 8.14 describes the test case for password change prompts.

Table 8.14   Password Change Prompt

Req. ID: STC-ATEN-009	Category: SECURITY
Subcategory(ies)/Tags	Authentication, Credentials, Login, Passwords
Name	Password Change Prompt
Description	Verify that the system provides notification to the user regarding the imminence of the password expiration.
Constraints	NA
Comments	This could be onscreen or even via e-mails and/or other channels.

Table 8.15 describes the test case for secure password changes.

Table 8.15   Secure Password Changes

Req. ID: STC-ATEN-010	Category: SECURITY
Subcategory(ies)/Tags	Authentication, Credentials, Login, Passwords
Name	Secure Password Changes
Description	Verify that the system forces reauthentication (with the current password/PIN) of the user at the time of an attempted change to password or PIN.
Constraints	NA
Comments	NA

Table 8.16 describes the test case for preventing password reuse.

Table 8.16   Preventing Password Reuse

Req. ID: STC-ATEN-011	Category: SECURITY
Subcategory(ies)/Tags	Authentication, Credentials, Login, Passwords
Name	Preventing Password Reuse
Description	■ Identify the implemented password policy for preventing reuse (e.g. last five passwords or all passwords used in the last 12 months) ■ Then, verify if the system has a mechanism to prevent the reuse of passwords within that period.
Constraints	NA
Comments	NA

Table 8.17 describes test case for password complexity.

Table 8.17   Password Complexity

Req. ID: STC-ATEN-012	Category: SECURITY
Subcategory(ies)/Tags	Authentication, Credentials, Login
Name	Password Complexity
Description	■ Verify that application has the administrative provisions to set password complexity requirements—for minimum length, alphabetic characters, and numeric or special characters. ■ Set several such complexity requirements and validate that they are being enforced for different user types.
Constraints	NA
Comments	When a complexity requirement changes, the new requirement must be automatically enforced during the next password change cycle.

Table 8.18 describes the test case for Configurable False Acceptance or Rejection.

Table 8.18   Configurable False Accept/Rejection

Req. ID: STC-ATEN-013	Category: SECURITY
Subcategory(ies)/Tags	Authentication, Credentials, Login, Biometrics
Name	Configurable False Accept/Rejection
Description	▪ Verify if the system supports administrator-configurable parameters to control false reject and false accept errors on biometric authentication systems. ▪ Set different values for each and validate if they are actually enforced for different user types with different sample datasets.
Constraints	NA
Comments	The final values have to be set based on organizational requirements, comprehensive testing, and risk assessment but the test has to be done for wide range of values.

Table 8.19 describes the test case for the protection of biometric authentication information.

Table 8.19   Protection of Biometric Authentication Information

Req. ID: STC-ATEN-014	Category: SECURITY
Subcategory(ies)/Tags	Authentication, Credentials, Login, Biometrics
Name	Protection of biometric authentication information
Description	▪ Verify if the system encrypts biometric authentication information during transmission and storage. ▪ Verify that the information stored can never be used to fully reconstruct the original information (e.g., fingerprint minutiae)[2]
Constraints	NA
Comments	A security expert in the area of biometrics security is recommended to perform these tests.

8.3   Test Cases for Authorization Requirements

This section lists the test cases for all the authorization requirements listed in Chapter 4.

Tables 8.20.1 through 8.20.3 describe the test case for access rights.

Table 8.20.1   Access Rights

Req. ID: STC-AUTR-001-1	Category: SECURITY
Subcategory(ies)/Tags	Authorization, Credentials, Access Control
Name	Access Rights 1
Description	Verify that the system does not allow access to system resources without checking the assigned rights and privileges of the authenticated user.
Constraints	NA
Comments	This has to be validated by trying out all the different parts (pages in web apps) of the application using different user IDs that have different privileges and ensuring that the expected behavior is exhibited.

Table 8.20.2   Access Rights

Req. ID: STC-AUTR-001-2	Category: SECURITY
Subcategory(ies)/Tags	Authorization, Credentials, Access Control
Name	Access Rights 2
Description	In case of Web applications, brute force access to different URLs to which to which particular users don't have access to is an important verification test.
Constraints	NA
Comments	This has to be validated by trying out all pages of the application using different user IDs which have different privileges and ensuring that the expected behavior is exhibited.

Table 8.20.3   Access Rights

Req. ID: STC-AUTR-001-3	Category: SECURITY
Subcategory(ies)/Tags	Authorization, Credentials, Access Control
Name	Access Rights 3
Description	In the case of Web applications, verify that no user-tamperable parameters/hidden parameters that control access control exist.
Constraints	NA
Comments	This has to be validated by trying out all the different pages of the application using different user IDs that have different privileges and ensuring that the expected behavior is exhibited.

Table 8.21 describes the test case for the protection of biometric authentication information

Table 8.21   Protection of Biometric Authentication Information

Req. ID: STC-AUTR-002	Category: SECURITY
Subcategory(ies)/Tags	Authorization, Credentials, Access Control, Biometrics
Name	Protection of biometric authentication information
Description	Verify that the system takes appropriate precautions, such as encryption/hashing, to protect authentication information while stored in the database.
Constraints	NA
Comments	This includes the representation of the user's personal characteristics (e.g., fingerprint, iris pattern).

Table 8.22 describes the test case for account lock-outs.

Table 8.22   Account Lock-Out

Req. ID: STC-AUTR-003	Category: SECURITY
Subcategory(ies)/Tags	Authorization, Credentials, Access Control, Authentication, Login
Name	Account Lock-Out
Description	If several consecutive incorrect login attempts are made, verify that the system generates an alarm and also locks out the account (for a specified period of time or indefinitely, depending on the criticality of the role and application) after an administrator-specifiable number of attempts.
Constraints	NA
Comments	The maximum default setting is three attempts.

Table 8.23 describes the test case for login banners.

Table 8.23   Login Banner

Req. ID: STC-AUTR-004	Category: SECURITY
Subcategory(ies)/Tags	Authorization, Credentials, Access Control
Name	Login Banner
Description	At the time of login and accessing system resources, verify that the system provides the capability to generate an administrator-configurable warning banner.
Constraints	NA
Comments	Similarly, since policies vary between organizations, it is necessary to verify the same test case for local customizations of the warning banner.

Table 8.24 describes the test case for last login information display.

Table 8.24 Last Login Information Display

Req. ID: STC-AUTR-005	Category: SECURITY
Subcategory(ies)/Tags	Authorization, Credentials, Access Control
Name	Last Login Information Display
Description	Upon successful login and session establishment, verify that the system displays the date and time of the last successful login.
Constraints	NA
Comments	NA

Table 8.25 describes the test case for session timeout.

Table 8.25 Session Timeout

Req. ID: STC-AUTR-006	Category: SECURITY
Subcategory(ies)/Tags	Session Management, Authorization, Authentication
Name	Session Timeout
Description	Verify that the system provides a "time-out" feature so that if during an active session there has not been any exchange of messages across the connection for an administrator-specified period of time, the system shall drop the connection and require a successful reauthentication to regain access.
Constraints	NA
Comments	This has to be tested on all interfaces of the application.

Table 8.26 describes the test case for access restriction.

Table 8.26 Access Restriction

Req. ID: STC-AUTR-007	Category: SECURITY
Subcategory(ies)/Tags	Authorization, Credentials, Access Control

Table 8.26   Access Restriction (continued)

Name	Access Restriction
Description	Verify that the system has the capability to restrict session establishment based on time-of-day, day-of-week, calendar date of the login, and source of the connection.
Constraints	NA
Comments	For Internet facing Web applications, this would include using geolocation information.

Table 8.27 describes the test case for user and group privileges.

Table 8.27   User and Group Privileges

Req. ID: STC-AUTR-008	Category: SECURITY
Subcategory(ies)/Tags	Authorization, Credentials, Access Control
Name	User and Group Privileges
Description	Verify that the system has administrative features to assign user and group privileges (i.e., access permissions) to user IDs (not authentication information).
Constraints	NA
Comments	

Table 8.28 describes the test case for role-based access control.

Table 8.28   Role-Based Access Control

Req. ID: STC-AUTR-009	Category: SECURITY
Subcategory(ies)/Tags	Authorization, Credentials, Access Control
Name	Role-Based Access Control (RBAC)
Description	Verify that the system provides an enforceable mechanism through which users can be segmented into roles (e.g., administrator) involving access to security features and other administrative functions.

Table 8.28　Role-Based Access Control

Constraints	NA
Comments	NA

Table 8.29 describes the test case for resource control mechanism.

Table 8.29　Resource Control Mechanism

Req. ID: STC-AUTR-010	Category: SECURITY
Subcategory(ies)/Tags	Authorization, Credentials, Access Control
Name	Resource Control Mechanism
Description	Verify that the system provides a resource control mechanism that grants or denies access to a resource based on user and interface privilege.
Constraints	NA
Comments	NA

Tables 8.30.1 and 8.30.2 describe the test case for concurrent logon sessions.

Table 8.30.1　Concurrent Logon Sessions

Req. ID: STC-AUTR-011-1	Category: SECURITY
Subcategory(ies)/Tags	Authorization, Credentials, Access Control, Session Management
Name	Concurrent Logon Sessions 1
Description	Verify that the system provides the capability for the administrator to specify limits on the number of concurrent logon sessions for a given user, the default value being one.
Constraints	NA
Comments	NA

Table 8.30.2   Concurrent Logon Sessions

Req. ID: STC-AUTR-011-2	Category: SECURITY
Subcategory(ies)/Tags	Authorization, Credentials, Access Control, Session Management
Name	Concurrent Logon Sessions 2
Description	Verify that administrator-specified limits on the number of concurrent logon sessions for a given user are actually enforced by using different user types and in all the interfaces to the application.
Constraints	NA
Comments	NA

8.3.1   Test Cases for Security Auditing Requirements

This section lists the test cases for all the Security Auditing requirements listed in Chapter 4.

Table 8.31 describes the test case for maintaining an audit log.

Table 8.31   Audit Log

Req. ID: STC-AUDT-001	Category: SECURITY
Subcategory(ies)/Tags	Audit, Forensics, Logging
Name	Audit Log
Description	Verify that the system maintains an audit log that provides adequate information for establishing audit trails on security breaches and user activity.
Constraints	NA
Comments	NA

Table 8.32 describes the test case for Logging of Authentication Information

Table 8.32   Logging of Authentication Information

Req. ID: STC-AUDT-002	Category: SECURITY
Subcategory(ies)/Tags	Audit, Forensics, Logging
Name	Logging of Authentication Information
Description	Verify that the system maintains the confidentiality of authenticators (e.g., passwords) by excluding them from being recorded in the audit log.
Constraints	NA
Comments	NA

Table 8.33 describes the test case for logging of specific events

Table 8.33   Logging of Specific Events

Req. ID: STC-AUDT-003	Category: SECURITY
Subcategory(ies)/Tags	Audit, Forensics, Logging
Name	Logging of Specific Events
Description	Verify that the system allows the administrator to configure the audit log to record specified events such as: ■ All sessions established ■ Failed user authentication attempts ■ Unauthorized attempts to access resources (e.g. software, data, process) ■ Administrator actions ■ Administrator disabling of audit logging ■ Events generated (e.g., commands issued) to make changes in users' security profiles and attributes ■ Events generated to make changes in the security profiles and attributes of system interfaces

Table 8.33   Logging of Specific Events

	▪ Events generated to make changes in permission levels needed to access a resource ▪ Events generated that make changes to the system security configuration ▪ Events generated that make modifications to the system software Verify that such events are actually logged by verifying the log location.
Constraints	NA
Comments	NA

Table 8.34 describes the test case for providing the ability to act on audit log failure.

Table 8.34   Action on Audit Log Failure

Req. ID: STC-AUDT-004	Category: SECURITY
Subcategory(ies)/Tags	Audit, Forensics, Logging
Name	Action on Audit Log Failure
Description	Verify that the system provides the administrator the ability to specify the appropriate actions to take (i.e., continue or terminate processing) when the audit log malfunctions or is terminated.
Constraints	NA
Comments	NA

Table 8.35 describes the test case for archival of audit logs.

Table 8.35   Archival of Audit Logs

Req. ID: STC-AUDT-005	Category: SECURITY
Subcategory(ies)/Tags	Audit, Forensics, Logging
Name	Archival of Audit Logs

Table 8.35 Archival of Audit Logs

Description	Verify that the system provides the administrator the ability to retrieve, print, and copy (to some long-term storage device) the contents of the audit log.
Constraints	NA
Comments	NA

Table 8.36 describes the test case for log review and reporting.

Table 8.36 Log Review and Reporting

Req. ID: STC-AUDT-006	Category: SECURITY
Subcategory(ies)/Tags	Audit, Forensics, Logging
Name	Log Review and Reporting
Description	Verify that the system provides administrators with audit analysis tools to selectively retrieve records from the audit log to perform functions such as producing reports, establishing audit trails, etc.
Constraints	NA
Comments	NA

Table 8.37 describes the test case for logging of specific information.

Table 8.37 Logging of Specific Information

Req. ID: STC-AUDT-007	Category: SECURITY
Subcategory(ies)/Tags	Audit, Forensics, Logging
Name	Logging of Specific Information

Table 8.37   Logging of Specific Information

Description	Verify that the system allows the administrator to configure the audit log to record specified information such as: ■ Date and time of the attempted event ■ Host name of the system generating the log record ■ User ID of the initiator of the attempted event ■ Names of resources accessed ■ Host name of the system that initiated the attempted event ■ Success or failure of the attempt (for the event) ■ Event type
Constraints	NA
Comments	NA

Table 8.38 describes the test case for protection of the audit log.

Table 8.38   Protection of Audit Log

Req. ID: STC-AUDT-008	Category: SECURITY
Subcategory(ies)/Tags	Audit, Forensics, Survivability
Name	Protection of Audit Log
Description	Verify that the system protects the audit log from unauthorized access, modification, or deletion. This protection shall be provided by assigning resource access permission to users and interfaces.
Constraints	NA
Comments	NA

8.3.2   Test Cases for Confidentiality Requirements

This section lists the test cases for all the confidentiality requirements listed in Chapter 4.

Table 8.39 describes the test case for protection of sensitive information.

Table 8.39   Sensitive Information Protection

Req. ID: STC-CONF-001	Category: SECURITY
Subcategory(ies)/Tags	Confidentiality, Data Protection, Information Disclosure, Cryptographic Keys
Name	Sensitive Information Protection
Description	Verify that the system has the capability to protect system-defined security-related and user-defined selected information from unauthorized disclosure while it is stored or in transit.
Constraints	NA
Comments	NA

Table 8.40 describes the test case for securing cryptographic keys.

Table 8.40   Cryptographic Key Security

Req. ID: STC-CONF-002	Category: SECURITY
Subcategory(ies)/Tags	Confidentiality, Data Protection, Information Disclosure, Cryptographic Keys
Name	Cryptographic Key Security
Description	If cryptographic keys are generated and stored, verify that the system provides secure key storage that is impractical to compromise through a logical or physical attack.
Constraints	NA
Comments	NA

Table 8.41 describes the test case for secure generation of strong cryptographic keys.

Table 8.41   Cryptographic Key Strength

Req. ID: STC-CONF-003	Category: SECURITY
Subcategory(ies)/Tags	Confidentiality, Data Protection, Information Disclosure, Cryptographic Keys
Name	Cryptographic Key Strength
Description	If cryptographic keys are generated, verify that the system implements a standard key generation algorithm that generates nonpredictable values.
Constraints	NA
Comments	NA

Table 8.42 describes the test case for cryptographic key expiration.

Table 8.42   Cryptographic Key Expiration

Req. ID: STC-CONF-004	Category: SECURITY
Subcategory(ies)/Tags	Confidentiality, Data Protection, Information Disclosure, Cryptographic Keys
Name	Cryptographic Key Expiration
Description	Verify that the system has the capability to enforce the administrator-specified time period for the validity of keys for a particular use and/or user and shall prevent further use of a key after it has expired.
Constraints	NA
Comments	NA

Table 8.43 describes the test case for cryptographic key revocation.

Table 8.43   Cryptographic Key Revocation

Req. ID: STC-CONF-005	Category: SECURITY
Subcategory(ies)/Tags	Confidentiality, Data Protection, Information Disclosure, Cryptographic Keys
Name	Cryptographic Key Revocation
Description	Verify that the system has the capability to enforce the immediate revocation of a user and the associated keying material when requested by the administrator.
Constraints	NA
Comments	NA

Table 8.44 describes the test case for cryptographic key recovery.

Table 8.44   Cryptographic Key Recovery

Req. ID: STC-CONF-006	Category: SECURITY
Subcategory(ies)/Tags	Confidentiality, Data Protection, Information Disclosure, Cryptographic Keys
Name	Cryptographic Key Recovery
Description	Verify that the system supports recovery of all encryption keys by an authorized and authenticated user.
Constraints	NA
Comments	NA

Table 8.45 describes another requirement for securing signing keys.

Table 8.45   Signing Key Security

Req. ID: STC-CONF-007	Category: SECURITY
Subcategory(ies)/Tags	Confidentiality, Data Protection, Information Disclosure, Cryptographic Keys
Name	Signing Key Security

Table 8.45   Signing Key Security (continued)

Description	Verify that the system does not use signing keys for purposes of data encryption.
Constraints	NA
Comments	NA

Table 8.46 describes the test case for securing signing keys.

Table 8.46   Security of Signing Keys

Req. ID: STC-CONF-008	Category: SECURITY
Subcategory(ies)/Tags	Confidentiality, Data Protection, Information Disclosure, Cryptographic Keys
Name	Security of Signing Keys
Description	Verify that the system does not allow for the third-party recovery of keys used to create digital signatures.
Constraints	NA
Comments	NA

8.3.3   Test Cases for Integrity Requirements

This section lists the test cases for all the integrity requirements listed in Chapter 4.

Table 8.47 describes the test case for integrity checking.

Table 8.47   Integrity Checking

Req. ID: STC-INTG-001	Category: SECURITY
Subcategory(ies)/Tags	Data Integrity, Data Protection
Name	Integrity Checking
Description	Verify that the system provides secure integrity checking capabilities through the interface between the user and the system and among systems.

Table 8.47   Integrity Checking (continued)

Constraints	NA
Comments	This would involve intercepting and tampering data during transmission. which may be applicable and tested only for sensitive and critical data.

Table 8.48 describes the test case for source identification.

Table 8.48   Source Identification

Req. ID: STC-INTG-002	Category: SECURITY
Subcategory(ies)/Tags	Data Integrity, Data Protection, Audit
Name	Source Identification
Description	Verify that the system has the capability to propagate, when requested, the original user identifier to the destination.
Constraints	NA
Comments	NA

Table 8.49 describes the test case for preserving header integrity.

Table 8.49   Header Integrity

Req. ID: STC-INTG-003	Category: SECURITY
Subcategory(ies)/Tags	Data Integrity, Data Protection
Name	Header Integrity
Description	Verify that the system provides mechanisms to preserve the integrity of protocol header information and user data.
Constraints	NA
Comments	NA

Table 8.50 describes the test case for protecting against replay attacks.

Table 8.50   Replay Attack Protection

Req. ID: STC-INTG-004	Category: SECURITY
Subcategory(ies)/Tags	Data Integrity, Data Protection, Immunity
Name	Replay Attack Protection
Description	Verify that the system provides mechanisms to detect communication security violations in real time, such as replay attacks that duplicate an authentic message.
Constraints	NA
Comments	NA

Table 8.51 describes the test case for integrity of sensitive information.

Table 8.51   Integrity of Sensitive Information

Req. ID: STC-INTG-005	Category: SECURITY
Subcategory(ies)/Tags	Data Integrity, Data Protection
Name	Integrity of Sensitive Information
Description	Verify that the system supports protocols that bind the integrity of sensitive information with the integrity of the associated protocol information.
Constraints	NA
Comments	NA

Table 8.52 describes the test case for protecting the integrity of logs.

Table 8.52   Integrity of Logs

Req. ID: STC-INTG-006	Category: SECURITY
Subcategory(ies)/Tags	Data Integrity, Data Protection, Logging
Name	Integrity of Logs

Table 8.52   Integrity of Logs

Description	Verify that the system has the capability to protect the integrity of audit log records by generating integrity checks (e.g., checksums or secure hashes) when the log records are created, and by verifying the integrity check data when the record is accessed.
Constraints	NA
Comments	NA

Table 8.53 describes the test case for providing integrity checks.

Table 8.53   Integrity Check

Req. ID: STC-INTG-007	Category: SECURITY
Subcategory(ies)/Tags	Data Integrity, Data Protection
Name	Integrity Checks
Description	Verify that the system has the capability to protect data integrity by performing data integrity checks; reject the data if the integrity check fails.
Constraints	NA
Comments	NA

8.3.4   Test Cases for Availability Requirements

This section lists the test cases for all the availability requirements listed in Chapter 4.

Table 8.54 describes the test case for secure scalability.

Table 8.54   Secure Scalability

Req. ID: STC-AVAL-001	Category: SECURITY
Subcategory(ies)/Tags	Scalability, Performance, Availability
Name	Secure Scalability

Table 8.54   Secure Scalability (continued)

Description	Verify that the system continues to operate securely when various operating parameters increase or decrease.
Constraints	NA
Comments	These operating parameters shall be specified by the Technology Provider in the Product Test Schedule and will be itemized in the Test Plan.

Table 8.55 describes the test case for capability to monitor availability.

Table 8.55   Capability to Monitor Availability

Req. ID: STC-AVAL-002	Category: SECURITY
Subcategory(ies)/Tags	System Integrity, System Maintenance, Availability
Name	Capability to Monitor Availability
Description	Verify that the system provides an administrator with the capability to monitor the state of availability of critical system resources (e.g., overflow indication, lost messages, and buffer queues).
Constraints	NA
Comments	NA

8.3.5   Test Cases for Nonrepudiation Requirements

This section lists the test cases for all the nonrepudiation requirements listed in Chapter 4.

Table 8.56 describes the test case for secure logging of specific information

Table 8.56   Secure Logging of Specific Information

Req. ID: STC-NREP-001	Category: SECURITY
Subcategory(ies)/Tags	Non-Repudiation, Logging, Accountability
Name	Secure Logging of Specific Information

Table 8.56   Secure Logging of Specific Information (continued)

Description	Verify that the system has the capability to securely record information related to the reception of specific information from a user or another system.
Constraints	NA
Comments	NA

Table 8.57 describes the test case for time stamping of messages

Table 8.57   Time Stamping

Req. ID: STC-NREP-002	Category: SECURITY
Subcategory(ies)/Tags	Nonrepudiation, Logging, Accountability
Name	Time Stamping
Description	Verify that the system has the capability to securely link received information with the originator of the information and other characteristics such as time and date.
Constraints	NA
Comments	NA

Table 8.58 describes the test case for digital signatures.

Table 8.58   Digital Signatures

Req. ID: STC-NREP-003	Category: SECURITY
Subcategory(ies)/Tags	Nonrepudiation, Logging, Accountability, Digital Signatures, Cryptographic Keys
Name	Digital Signatures
Description	Verify that the system has the capability to interface with a specified trusted third party to obtain cryptographic keys that will link the received information or request with a specific user.
Constraints	NA
Comments	NA

8.3.6   Test Cases for Immunity Requirements

This section lists the test cases for all the immunity requirements listed in Chapter 4.

Table 8.59 describes the default denial requirements.

Table 8.59   Default Deny

Req. ID: STC-IMMU-001	Category: SECURITY
Subcategory(ies)/Tags	Authorization, Credentials, Access Control, Immunity
Name	Default Deny
Description	Verify that the system denies the access unless a user has permission to access a resource.
Constraints	NA
Comments	NA

Table 8.60 describes the test case for scope limitation.

Table 8.60   Scope Limitation

Req. ID: STC-IMMU-002	Category: SECURITY
Subcategory(ies)/Tags	Authorization, Credentials, Access Control, Immunity
Name	Scope Limitation
Description	Verify that the system provides the ability to define system level or administrative privileges with appropriate scope limitations.
Constraints	NA
Comments	These scope limitations must be clearly documented based on security review of the application.

Table 8.61 describes the requirement to limit execution of potentially damaging commands.

Table 8.61   Limit Execution

Req. ID: STC-IMMU-003	Category: SECURITY
Subcategory(ies)/Tags	Authorization, Credentials, Access Control, Immunity
Name	Limit Execution
Description	Verify that the system has the capability to prevent access to potentially damaging commands (e.g., delete all files) from users who do not need to execute such commands on a regular basis and from interfaces that are not intended to be used for such commands.
Constraints	NA
Comments	NA

Table 8.62 describes the test case for Create, Read, Update, and Delete (CRUD)–based access control.

Table 8.62   CRUD-Based Access Control

Req. ID: STC-IMMU-004	Category: SECURITY
Subcategory(ies)/Tags	Authorization, Credentials, Access Control, Immunity
Name	CRUD-Based Access Control
Description	Verify that the system has the capability to impose access control on the basis of functions such as Create, Read, Update, and Delete (CRUD).
Constraints	NA
Comments	NA

8.3.7   Test Cases for Survivability Requirements

This section lists the test cases for all the survivability requirements listed in Chapter 4.

Table 8.63 describes the test case for buffer overflow protection.

Table 8.63   Buffer Overflow Protection

Req. ID: STC-SURV-001	Category: SECURITY
Subcategory(ies)/Tags	System Integrity, System Maintenance, Survivability
Name	Buffer Overflow Protection
Description	Verify that the system prevents buffer overflow conditions that allow for unauthorized access by using dynamic analysis tools, static analysis tools, and fuzz testing tools.
Constraints	NA
Comments	NA

Table 8.64 describes the test case for log malfunction alerting.

Table 8.64   Log Malfunction Alert

Req. ID: STC-SURV-002	Category: SECURITY
Subcategory(ies)/Tags	Audit, Forensics, Survivability
Name	Log Malfunction Alert
Description	Verify whether the system generates a real-time alarm and has the capability to send an e-mail notification for impeding failures (running out of storage space) or if the audit log malfunctions is shut down for any reason.
Constraints	NA
Comments	NA

Table 8.65 describes the test case for logging through system restarts.

Table 8.65   Logging through System Restarts

Req. ID: STC-SURV-003	Category: SECURITY
Subcategory(ies)/Tags	Data Integrity, Audit, Forensics, Logging, Survivability

Table 8.65   Logging through System Restarts (continued)

Name	Logging through System Restarts
Description	Verify whether the system allows the audit log and its control mechanisms to maintain integrity and completeness through system restarts.
Constraints	NA
Comments	NA

8.3.8   Test Cases for Systems Maintenance Security Requirements

This section lists the test cases for all the Systems Maintenance Security requirements listed in Chapter 4.

Table 8.66 describes the test case for source tracking.

Table 8.66   Source Tracking

Req. ID: STC-SYSM-001	Category: SECURITY
Subcategory(ies)/Tags	System Integrity, System Maintenance, Forensics
Name	Source Tracking
Description	For software and data created or modified in the system, verify that the system provides an administrator with the capability to retrieve the user ID along with the date and time associated with that creation or modification.
Constraints	NA
Comments	NA

Table 8.67 describes the test case for system integrity checks.

Table 8.67   System Integrity Checks

Req. ID: STC-SYSM-002	Category: SECURITY
Subcategory(ies)/Tags	System Integrity, System Maintenance
Name	System Integrity Checks

Table 8.67 System Integrity Checks (continued)

Description	Verify if the system provides an administrator with the capability to perform integrity checks (e.g., synchronization points, checksums) on system data and software.
Constraints	NA
Comments	NA

Table 8.68 describes the test case for system snapshot reporting.

Table 8.68 System Snapshot Report

Req. ID: STC-SYSM-003	Category: SECURITY
Subcategory(ies)/Tags	System Integrity, System Maintenance
Name	System Snapshot Report
Description	Verify that the system provides the administrator with the capability to generate a system snapshot report detailing the values of the parameters and flags that affect secure operation of the system.
Constraints	NA
Comments	NA

Table 8.69 describes the test case for secure system recovery.

Table 8.69 Secure Recovery

Req. ID: STC-SYSM-004	Category: SECURITY
Subcategory(ies)/Tags	System Integrity, System Maintenance
Name	Secure Recovery
Description	Verify that the system provides an administrator with the capability to perform secure recovery.
Constraints	NA
Comments	NA

Table 8.70 describes the test case for security data backup and restore.

Table 8.70   Security Data Backup/Restore

Req. ID: STC-SYSM-005	Category: SECURITY
Subcategory(ies)/Tags	System Integrity, System Maintenance
Name	Security Data Backup/Restore
Description	Verify that the system provides an administrator with the capability to back up and restore all security-relevant data, such as system configurations, user profiles, and access permissions.
Constraints	NA
Comments	NA

Table 8.71 describes the test case for checking the integrity of security data from backup sources.

Table 8.71   Restore from Backup Checks

Req. ID: STC-SYSM-006	Category: SECURITY
Subcategory(ies)/Tags	System Integrity, System Maintenance
Name	Restore from Backup Checks
Description	Verify that the system has the capability to check the integrity of security data read from a back up file when performing a restore function.
Constraints	NA
Comments	NA

Table 8.72 describes the test case for security setting recovery.

Table 8.72   Security Settings Recovery

Req. ID: STC-SYSM-007	Category: SECURITY
Subcategory(ies)/Tags	System Integrity, System Maintenance
Name	Security Settings Recovery

Table 8.72   Security Settings Recovery (continued)

Description	Verify that the system securely recovers all of the security settings and stored security parameters during the normal recovery operation.
Constraints	NA
Comments	NA

Table 8.73 describes the test case for retaining security parameters through system restarts.

Table 8.73   Security Parameters through System Restarts

Req. ID: STC-SYSM-008	Category: SECURITY
Subcategory(ies)/Tags	System Integrity, System Maintenance
Name	Security Parameters through System Restarts
Description	Verify that the system retains the existing security parameters even after a restart or recovery.
Constraints	NA
Comments	NA

8.4   Summary

In Chapter 8, you saw dozens of test cases for the software security requirements in Chapter 4. These are intended for you to reuse and customize as you're preparing system specification documents and testing plans for each application you're developing. By using these, along with the documented requirements you help to assure that security requirements won't be dropped or treated as second-class citizens.

In Chapter 9, you'll find detailed information on security testing methods and some of the best practices people have found as useful and practical.

1.   "Backdoor (Computing): Reflections on Trusting Trust," Wikipedia, accessed May 8, 2011, http://en.wikipedia.org/wiki/Backdoor_(computing)#Reflections_on_Trusting_Trust.

2.   Arun Ross, Jidnya Shah, and Anil K. Jain, "Towards Reconstructing Fingerprints from Minutiae Points," accessed May 10, 2011, www.csee.wvu.edu/~ross/pubs/RossReconstruct_SPIE05.pdf.

Chapter 9

Testing Methods and Best Practices

In Chapter 8 you saw a rather large set of test cases to validate that the security requirements you demanded were *actually* implemented. We also looked at a possible common policy framework to codify test cases for simple import into different security testing tools.

In this chapter, you'll find testing methods and best practices for assuring that security features are present and operating as you intended.

9.1 Secure Testing Approach

Not all applications are created equal.

Software applications range from simple brochureware to mission-critical applications that are the lifeblood of a company. Given this, the first step is to determine a security testing approach and apply the right levels of testing based on the type of application.

While multiple application-risk ranking methodologies are out there, the Open Web Application Security Project (OWASP) Application Security Verification Standard (ASVS)[1] establishes a cogent and practical approach to security testing that anyone can apply.

9.2 OWASP's Application Security Verification Standard (ASVS)

The primary goal of the OWASP Application Security Verification Standard (ASVS) project is to normalize the range of coverage and level of rigor available in the marketplace for performing Web application security verification. The standard serves as the basis for testing application technical security controls, as well as any technical security controls that already exist in the environment.

ASVS defines verification and documentation requirements that are grouped on the basis of related coverage and level of rigor. The standard defines four levels and several sublevels:

- Level 1—Automated Verification
    - Level 1A—Dynamic Scan (Partial Automated Verification)
    - Level 1B—Source Code Scan (Partial Automated Verification)
- Level 2—Manual Verification
    - Level 2A—Security Test (Partial Manual Verification)
    - Level 2B—Code Review (Partial Manual Verification)
- Level 3—Design Verification
- Level 4—Internal Verification

Web application security verification is performed by analyzing the application logic into and out of a target application, which ASVS refers to as the Target of Verification or TOV.

Figure 9.1 below illustrates the ASVS levels and their relationship to testing techniques.

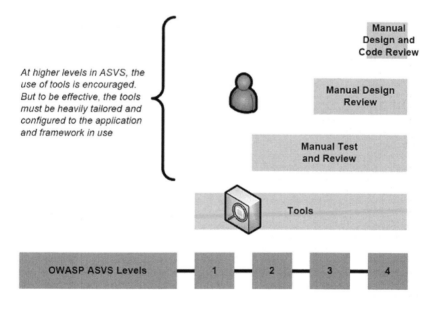

Figure 9.1   ASVS Levels and Testing Techniques (Source: OWASP)

More complex applications require more time to analyze, resulting in longer and more costly verifications. Lines of code are not the only factors that determine the complexity of an application–different technologies will typically require different amounts of analysis. Simple applications may include software libraries and frameworks. Applications of moderate complexity may include simple Web 1.0 applications. Complex applications may include Web 2.0 applications and new or unique Web technologies and technology combinations.

ASVS defines constituent components for Levels 1 and 2 (e.g. verification at Level 1 requires meeting both Level 1A and 1B requirements). For example, applications may claim conformance to either Level 1A or 1B instead of Level 1, but such a claim is weaker than claiming complete Level 1 conformance.

Verification and documentation requirements are defined using three types of requirements:

- High-level requirement
- Detailed requirements
- Reporting requirements

The high-level requirements define the overall application implementation and verification requirements. The detailed requirements define low-level application implementation and verification requirements (i.e., specific items to verify). The reporting requirements define how the results of performing an application verification using OWASP ASVS must be documented.

9.2.1   Application Security Verification Levels

The ASVS levels increase in both breadth and depth as one moves up through the levels. The breadth is defined in each level by a set of security requirements that must be addressed. The depth of the verification is defined by the approach and level of rigor required in verifying each security requirement.

Tools are an important part of every ASVS level. At higher levels in ASVS, the use of tools is encouraged. But to be effective, the tools must be heavily tailored and configured to the application and frameworks in use. At all levels, tool results must be manually verified.

It is a verifier's responsibility to determine if a TOV meets all of the requirements at the level targeted by a review. If the application meets all of the requirements for that level, then it can be considered an *OWASP ASVS Level N application*, in which *N* is the verification level where the verifier

determined conformance. If the application does not meet all the requirements for a particular level but does meet all the requirements for a lower
level of this standard, then it can be considered to have passed the lower
level of verification.

9.2.2   Level 1—Automated Verification

Level 1 (Automated Verification) is typically appropriate for applications
where some confidence in the correct use of security controls is required.
Threats to security will typically be viruses and worms (targets are chosen
indiscriminately through wide scans and impact the most vulnerable). The
scope of verification includes code that was developed or modified in order
to create the application.

In Level 1, the verification involves the use of automated tools aug-
mented with manual verification. This level only provides partial application security verification coverage. The manual verification here is only used
to verify that each automated tool finding is real and not a false positive.

There are two constituent components for Level 1:

- Level 1A is for the use of automated application vulnerability scanning (dynamic analysis) tools.
- Level 1B is for the use of automated source code scanning (static
  analysis) tools.

Verification efforts may use either of these components individually, or
may perform a combination of these approaches to achieve a complete Level
1 conformance rating.

For an application to meet Level 1 conformance, it must meet both
Level 1A and 1B requirements.

9.2.3   Level 2—Manual Verification

Level 2 (Manual Verification) is appropriate for applications that handle
personal transactions, conduct business-to-business transactions, process
credit card information, or process personally identifiable information
(PII). Level 2 provides some confidence in the correct use of security controls and confidence that the security controls are working correctly.
Threats to security are typically viruses, worms, and unsophisticated
opportunists such as attackers with professional or open-source attack tools
(script kiddies). The scope of verification includes all code developed or

modified for the application, as well as examining the security of all third-party components that provide security functions for the application.

While it may be determined that an application meets either Level 2A or 2B, neither of these levels alone provide the same levels of rigor or coverage as Level 2 combined. Further, while Level 2 is a superset of Level 1, there is no requirement to run an automated tool to meet the Level 2 requirements, since they may have already been run for Level 1 conformance. Instead, the verifier has the option of using just manual techniques for all requirements. If automated tool results are available, the verifier may use them to support the analysis. However, even passing a requirement at Level 1 does not automatically indicate passing the same requirement at Level 2. This is because automated tools provide insufficient evidence that the security control requirement has been fully met.

Manual techniques may still employ the use of tools. These can include the use of any kind of security analysis or testing tool, including the automated tools that are used for Level 1 verifications. However, such tools are simply *aids to the analyst* to find and assess the security controls being tested.

9.2.4   Level 3—Design Verification

Level 3 (Design Verification) is typically appropriate for applications that handle significant business-to-business transactions, including those that process healthcare information, implement business-critical or sensitive functions, or process other sensitive assets. Threats to security will typically be viruses and worms, opportunists, and possibly determined attackers (skilled and motivated attackers focusing on specific targets using tools, including purpose-built and bespoke scanning tools). The scope of verification includes all code developed or modified for the application, as well as examining the security of all third-party components that provide security functions for the application. Level 3 conformance assures that security controls themselves are working correctly, and that security controls everywhere within the application are used to enforce application-specific policies.

At Level 3, application components may be defined in terms of either individual or groups of source files, libraries, and/or executables that are grouped into a high-level architecture (for example MVC components, business function components, and data layer components). At Level 3, supporting threat modeling information about threat agents and assets must be provided. The path (or paths) a given end-user request may take through a high-level view of the application must be documented, as

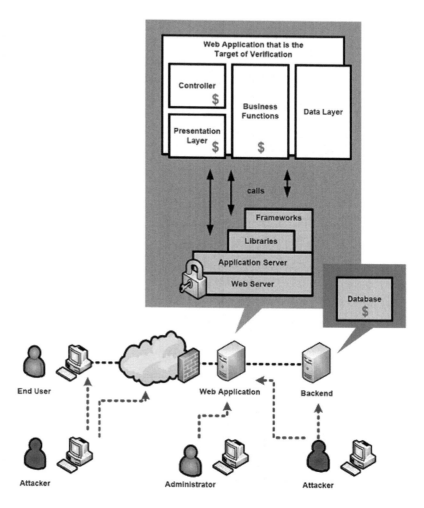

Figure 9.2   ASVS Level 3 Path Analysis ($ Indicates Assets) (Source: OWASP)

depicted in Figure 9.2. At Level 3, all potential paths through the high-level view of the application must be examined.

9.2.5   Level 4—Internal Verification

Level 4 (Internal Verification) is typically appropriate for critical applications that protect life and safety, critical infrastructure, or defense functions. Level 4 may also be appropriate for applications that process sensitive assets. Level 4 ensures that security controls themselves are working correctly, that security controls are used everywhere within the application needed to enforce application-specific policies, and that secure coding practices were followed.

Threats to security will be from determined attackers (skilled and motivated attackers focusing on specific targets using tools including purpose-built and bespoke scanning tools). The scope of verification expands beyond the scope of Level 3 to include all code used by the application.

At Level 4, the application's architecture is be captured as required at Level 3. Further, Level 4 requires that *all application code*, including unexamined code, be identified as part of the application definition, as depicted

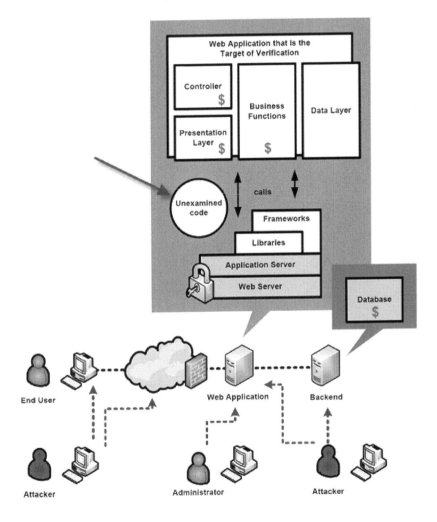

Figure 9.3   ASVS Unexamined Code Example ($ Indicates Assets) (Source: OWASP)

in Figure 9.3. This code must include all libraries, frameworks, and supporting code that the application relies on. Previous verifications of these components can be reused. Platform code, such as the operating system, virtual machine, or core libraries issued with a virtual machine environment, Web server, or application server are not included in Level 4.

9.2.6   Security Testing Methods

Now that you've seen the different levels as described by ASVS, we'll switch to examining the four key methods of security testing prescribed by ASVS:

1.   Manual Source Code Review
2.   Automated Source Code Analysis
3.   Automated Dynamic Analysis
4.   Penetration Testing

9.3   Manual Source Code Review

Manual source code reviews can begin when there is sufficient code from the development process to review. The scope of a source code review is usually limited to finding code-level problems that could potentially result in security vulnerabilities. Code reviews are *not* used to reveal:

- Problems related to business requirements that cannot be implemented securely
- Issues with the selection of a particular technology for the application
- Design issues that might result in vulnerabilities

Source code reviews typically are not concerned about the *exploitability* of vulnerabilities. Findings from the review are treated just like any other defects found by other methods, and they are handled in the same ways. Code reviews are also useful for nonsecurity findings that can affect the overall code quality. Code reviews typically result in the identification of not only security problems but also dead code, redundant code, unnecessary complexity, or any other violation of the best practices we described earlier in the book. Each of the findings carries its own priority, which is typically defined in the organization's *bug priority matrix*. Bug reports often contain a specific remediation recommendation by the reviewer so that the developer can fix it appropriately.

Manual code reviews are expensive because they involve many manual efforts and often involve security specialists to assist in the review. However, manual reviews have proven their value repeatedly when it comes to accuracy and quality. They also help to identify logic vulnerabilities that typically cannot be identified by automated static code analyzers.

Source code reviews are often called *white box* analyses. This is because the reviewer has complete internal knowledge of the design, threat models, and other system documentation for the application. *Black box* analysis, on the other hand, is performed from an outsider's view of the application with no access to specifications or knowledge of the application's inner workings. *Gray box* analysis is somewhere in between white box and black box analysis, as you will see later in this chapter.

9.4   Automated Source Code Analysis

Medium-to-large enterprises cannot afford to complete a manual code review on every single application every single time. Instead, many rely on automated source code analyzers to help.

Typical software development priorities are schedule, cost, features and then quality—in most cases, in that order. The pressure from a time-to-market perspective can negatively affect software quality and resilience and sometimes causes the postponement of adding features to the software.

As Phillip Crosby said, "Quality is free,"[2] and this is most true of the software development process. However, managers in organizations that do software development often believe otherwise: They appear to think that a focus on software quality increases costs and delays projects. Studies of software quality (not necessarily software security) consistently prove this belief wrong.

Organizations with a mature SDLC process usually face little extra overhead because of software quality and resilience requirements, and the corresponding cost savings from process improvements far exceed the cost of added developer activities.

Static source code analyzers support the secure development of programs in an organization by finding and listing the potential security bugs in the code base. They provide a wide variety of views/reports and trends on the security posture of the code base and can be used as an effective mechanism to collect metrics that indicate the progress and maturity of the software security activities. Source code analyzers operate in short time frames that would otherwise require several thousand person-hours to complete if they were done manually. Automated tools also provide risk rankings for each vulnerability, which helps the organization to prioritize its remediation strategies.

Most important, automated code analyzers help an organization uncover defects earlier in the SDLC, enabling cost and reputation savings.

9.4.1 Automated Reviews Compared with Manual Reviews

Although automated source code analyzers are strong at performing with low incremental costs, are good at catching the typical low-hanging fruits, have an ability to scale to several thousands of lines of code, and are good at performing repetitive tasks quickly, they also have some drawbacks . . .

Automated tools tend to report a high number of false positives. Sometimes it will take an organization several months to fine-tune the tool to reduce these false positives, but some level of noise will always remain in the findings. Source code analyzers are poor at detecting business logic flaws. Some of the other types of attacks that automated analysis cannot detect are complex information leakage, design flaws, subjective vulnerabilities such as cross-site request forgery, sophisticated race conditions, and multistep-process attacks.

In a research paper written by James Kupsch and Barton Miller of the University of Wisconsin, the authors presented the results of their efforts to evaluate and quantify the effectiveness of automated source code vulnerability assessment tools by comparing such tools to the results of an in-depth manual evaluation of the same system.[3] The key findings were the following:

- Of the 15 serious vulnerabilities found in the study, Fortify Software found six and Coverity only one.
- Both Fortify and Coverity had significant false positive rates, with Coverity having a lower false positive rate. The volumes of these false positives were significant enough to have a serious impact on the effectiveness of the analyst.
- In the Fortify and Coverity results, they found no significant vulnerabilities beyond those identified by the study.

9.4.2 Automated Source Code Analysis Tools—Deployment Strategy

While there are any number of strategies to scan source code using any of these scanners, we strongly recommend a two-pronged approach to the deployment model: an integrated development environment (IDE)–based integration for developers and a build process–based integration for application development governance and management.

9.4.3   IDE Integration for Developers

To help developers scan the code that they write early enough in the life cycle, you need to provide them with unfettered access to automated scanning tool(s) so that they can perform scans themselves, right at their desktops, through an IDE.

Scanning can be performed on a single function or method, on a file or a collection of source code files, or on the entire application system. This self-service scan will provide results that developers can use directly to clean up their code based on the findings. A report typically provides generic recommendations on how to fix the identified vulnerabilities.

There is usually no need to track the metrics from these scan results, because the code is usually too early in its life cycle to be measured. One key metric to track, however, is the raw number and percentage of adoption of the IDE scanning by the development community–by sheer count and also by the number of projects they submit to the tool for scanning.

9.4.4   Build Integration for Governance

Build process–based scanning occurs when the entire application (all modules and libraries) are ready to be built and tested. This typically includes source code components coming in from different development teams and even different software development companies (e.g., outsourced development.)

This centralized scanning is meant as a governance and management mechanism and provides gating criteria before the code is released to production. This scanning happens along with the other tests in the quality-assurance or user-acceptance test phases, and the test team reports back to the developers the bugs identified for fixing. Typical gating criteria for production movement might state:

- Zero high-risk vulnerabilities
- No more than five medium-risk vulnerabilities
- No more than ten low-risk vulnerabilities, etc.

You should use the build process–based scanning not only for planned software releases but also for emergency bug fixes. Since the scanning process is closely integrated with the build process, automation takes care of assuring that source code scanning happens every time.

When the assurance level of the automated scanner is high (not too many false positives), then the build server can be triggered to fail the build based on the gating criteria from above.

Metrics that are useful to track for measuring performance and progress include:

- KLOC (thousands of lines of code) scanned
- Percent of lines of code (LOC) within the entire application that are scanned
- LOC scanned/unit time
- Number and percent of applications scanned using IDE scan
- Number and percent of applications scanned using build scan
- Number and percent of applications scanned using build scan that failed/passed
- Vulnerability density (vulnerability/KLOC)
- Vulnerability severity comparison across projects or development teams
- Vulnerability category comparison across projects or development teams
- Vulnerability category specific trending
- Average time taken to close high/medium/low-risk vulnerabilities
- Vulnerability distribution by project
- Top ten vulnerabilities by severity and frequency

9.4.5   Automated Dynamic Analysis

Similar to the automated analysis of source code, you can carry out automated dynamic analysis, which is sometimes referred to as black box testing. Black box application security testing tools have a "Web spider" that crawls the application and learns about its characteristics.

After this preanalysis phase, the tools load up several thousand test cases with different malicious payloads that are relevant to that application. Then these test cases are executed and the malicious requests are sent to the application, and the response from the application is observed and analyzed to see whether there are any potential vulnerabilities.

Black box testing helps to identify potential security vulnerabilities within commercial and proprietary applications when the source code is not available for review and analysis. Many organizations use this type of scanning to qualify new products in their software procurement process.

Most tools look for and report on the following vulnerabilities:

- Improper input validation
- Command injection and buffer overflow attacks
- SQL injection attacks
- Cross-site scripting vulnerabilities
- Cross-site request forgeries
- Directory traversal attacks
- Improper session management
- Improper authorization and access control mechanisms

9.4.6 Limitations of Automated Dynamic Analysis Tools

For automated testing on an entire system, it is often required that the testing tool be able to log in to the application, just as an end user would to access the "juicy" parts of the program or system. Let us use an e-banking application as an example. For any nontrivial features of the application (e.g., paying bills, checking balances, applying for loans or credit cards), a login is required so the application can properly identify the customer and only provide information related to that customer's accounts. Pen testing tools require the same access if they are being used to access the security of protected Web forms and functions. Most products allow you to configure the credentials needed, but it is vital that the test accounts that are used for logging in are reflective enough of real-life data; otherwise the tests may be incomplete or unable to reach parts of an application that a normal user would. As a result, it is critical that the test environment mirror the production environment as much as possible, and since testing in production is a universal violation of security best practices and most regulations, you have little choice but to ensure that your QA testing environment can behave nearly identically to your production environment, without the risks of using actual, live data for testing purposes.

9.4.7 Automated Dynamic Analysis Tools—Deployment Strategy

Since many people consider automated security testing tools "too risky" in the hands of a malicious insider, organizations typically restrict their availability to only the security team or the quality assurance team. Just as a car can be used for good or evil, black box testing tools can either help an organization with their software security or turn them into a victim of a malicious user intending as much harm possible in the shortest period of time possible without being caught.

Some of the commercial tools provide restricted Web-based access to developers in order to scan specific IP addresses where their test applications under development are deployed, without allowing access to production network segments. Such tools provide for restricted developer testing during development, while other configurations are used for centralized QA testing for governance and management of the software development life cycle.

9.4.8   Developer Testing

For Web applications when the application development architecture and development methodology permit, providing restricted access to a black box scanning tool to the developers of the application might be recommended. This way, they can test for security vulnerabilities earlier in the life cycle and avoid security bugs entering the integration or build testing phases, similar to the deployment of source code analyzers in the same environment. Just be sure that developers cannot reach the production network from the network segment where testing occurs.

9.4.9   Centralized Quality Assurance Testing

Apart from providing developers access to the black box tool, the quality assurance (QA) team or the testing team should also have access to these tools. The testing carried out by this independent team might also serve as gating criteria for promoting the application QA testing and production environments. The results from these test results should be shared with the developers quickly after the tests are run, so they can develop strategies for fixing the problems that are uncovered. Once the criteria for moving to production are met, the QA team should sign off on the security vulnerability testing, along with the other test results (functional testing, user acceptance testing, etc.).

Centralized penetration testing also ensures that other minor feature additions and bug fixes are also tested for security bugs before they too are moved to production.

9.5 Penetration (Pen) Testing

Pen testing involves actively attacking and analyzing the behavior of a deployed application or network devices. The Open Source Security Testing Methodology Manual (OSSTMM)[4] is a peer-reviewed methodology for performing security tests and metrics. The OSSTMM test cases are divided into five channels (sections) which collectively test:

- Information and data controls
- Personnel security awareness levels
- Fraud and social engineering control levels
- Computer and telecommunications networks
- Wireless devices, mobile devices
- Physical security access controls, security processes, and physical locations such as buildings, perimeters, and military bases

For the purposes of this chapter, we can restrict ourselves to security testing to software applications. Penetration testing is performed from the perspective of an outside attacker (one who has no inside knowledge of the application) and involves exploiting identified vulnerabilities to break the system or gain access to unauthorized information. The intent of a penetration test is not only to identify potential vulnerabilities but also to determine exploitability of an attack and the degree of business impact of a successful exploit.

Black box testing is the set of activities that occurs during the predeployment test phase or on a periodic basis after a system has been deployed. Security experts perform this testing with the help of automated tools and/or manual penetration testing. Many organizations conduct black box tests to comply with regulatory requirements (e.g. PCI DSS compliance), protect their customers' confidential and sensitive information, and protect the organization's brand and reputation.

A manual penetration test involves humans actually attacking the system by sending malicious requests and carefully inspecting every single response. They carry out the testing "by hand," with or without the help of penetration testing software, but they do not rely on the automated tester to perform all the work.

The most significant advantage of manual penetration testing is the ability to discover business logic vulnerabilities. The obvious drawback is that it is costly and time-consuming, since it requires humans with specialized skills to perform.

9.5.1   Gray Box Testing

A combination of black box testing and white box testing, referred to as gray box testing, is the most widely used methodology by organizations that want a high level of assurance in their security testing processes. A team of security experts is engaged to review the design and source code for an "inside-out" view of the application. A review and analysis of the application from a hacker's perspective provides the "outside-in" view of the application. The security team analyzes and correlates the results from both types of reviews and eliminates possible false positives. You need both types of reviews for assurance that a secure and resilient application development methodology is present and working as you intended.

9.6   Summary

In Chapter 9 we covered the various levels of testing and approach to testing as described by the OWASP ASVS. We then looked at the different types of testing methods, comparisons between them, their constraints, metrics, and also usage and deployments strategies. While there is no single tool or technique that can uncover all security-related problems or issues–there are no silver bullets–when it comes to software security, you need to pick the right combination and approaches based on the required security assurance levels for all application software you develop or commission for development.

9.7   References

1. "OWASP Application Security Verification Standard Project,"OWASP: The Open Web Application Security Project Web site, accessed April 16, 2011, https://www.owasp.org/index.php/Category:OWASP_Application_Security_Verification_Standard_Pr oject.

2. Crosby, P., *Quality Is Free*, Mentor Publishing, 1980.

3. James A. Kupsch and Barton P. Miller, "Manual vs. Automated Vulnerability Assessment: A Case Study," accessed April 17, 2011, http://pages.cs.wisc.edu/~kupsch/va/ManVsAutoVulnAssessment.pdf.

4. "OSSTM–Open Source Security Testing Methodology Manual," ISECOM: Institute for Security and Open Methodologies Web site, accessed April 17, 2011, www.isecom.org/osstmm.M

Chapter 10

Connecting the Moving Parts

Over the last nine chapters, you were given a bounty of software requirements, new ways of thinking about software development, tools, techniques, and processes to improve the security and resilience of custom built applications. In Chapter 10, we'll pull all the moving parts together to help you build a roadmap for applying these practices and content into a cohesive collection of activities. At this point you've learned:

- Why good requirements and design are the keys to a successful software development effort, and how finding and fixing defects early in the lifecycle saves you time and money
- The importance of nonfunctional requirements (NFRs) and the SQUARE methodology
- Resilience and quality considerations for application software and the application runtime environment
- The value of a set of reusable generic security requirements for application software
- Which security services are best *pushed down* into the operating environment as infrastructure services that are published with open interfaces for gaining access to the service
- Design principles for secure and resilient applications and the infrastructure that supports software operations
- Best practices used to convert requirements into secure software designs
- Test cases for the documented security requirements
- Testing methods and best practices for ensuring that security features are present and operating as intended

While we don't advocate that every development project use all 93 documented security requirements every time, we do recommend that a thorough risk analysis of the proposed application be conducted to best understand the threats your application will need to counter. There may be instances where all 93 security requirements do make the most sense–if you're developing a security tool (e.g., firewall software, access controls, etc.), you may in fact need to counter every threat that the documented requirements address.

The point is, developers will not magically incorporate security and resilience into an application unless they're explicitly told to include them. While you can achieve this by documenting every requirement into your systems analysis documentation, you can also achieve it by letting the developers know what types of security testing they can expect for the applications they're building. Simply documenting a requirement that states "The application shall be developed securely" is insufficient, since each developer will interpret that in his or her own way. A better bet is to let the developers know know long before development begins about the types of testing their applications will be expected to pass before it's accepted as final.

In Chapter 9 we examined the OWASP's Application Security Verification Standard (ASVS) project as one way to determine the level of testing required for an application based on a host of factors, but to connect functional and nonfunctional requirements to development to verification to deployment, we need to take a more comprehensive look at the secure software development lifecycle. For that we turn to the Open Software Assurance Maturity Model (OpenSAMM) to fill in the gaps.

10.1   OpenSAMM

OpenSAMM is an open framework, also developed as an Open Web Application Security Project (OWASP) for helping organizations to formulate and implement a *strategy* for software security that is tailored to specific risks facing the organization.[1] OpenSAMM offers a roadmap and well-defined maturity model for secure software development and deployment, along with useful tools for self-assessment and planning.

The resources provided by OpenSAMM will aid in:

- Evaluating an organization's existing software security practices
- Building a balanced software security program in well-dened iterations
- Demonstrating concrete improvements to a security assurance program
- Dening and measuring security-related activities within an organization

SAMM was defined with flexibility that provides utility by small, medium, and large organizations that use any type of SDLC. The model can be applied organizationwide, for a single line of business, or even on an individual project.

OpenSAMM starts with the core activities that should be present in any organization that develops software:

- Governance
- Construction
- Verication
- Deployment

In each of these core activities, three security practices are defined for 12 practices that are used to determine the overall maturity of your program. The security practices cover all areas relevant to software security assurance, and each provides a "silo" for improvement. Each of the 12 Security Practices has 3 defined Maturity Levels and an implicit starting point at zero. The details for each level differ between the practices, but they generally represent:

0   Implicit starting point representing the activities in the Practice being unfulfilled

1   Initial understanding and ad hoc provision of Security Practice

2   Increase efficiency and/or effectiveness of the Security Practice

3   Comprehensive mastery of the Security Practice at scale

The three security practices for each level of core activities are shown in Figure 10.1.

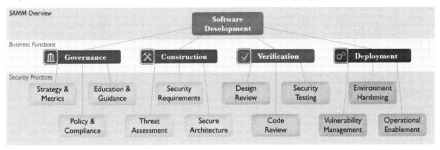

Figure 10.1   OpenSAMM Security Practice (Source: SAMM 1.0, p. 3)

Governance is focused on the processes and activities that are related to *how* an organization manages overall software development activities. Specifically, this includes concerns that cross-cut groups involved in application development as well as business processes that are established at the organization level.

Construction concerns the processes and activities related to how an organization defines goals and creates software within development projects. In general, this includes product management, requirements gathering, high-level architecture specifications, detailed design, and implementation.

Verification is focused on the processes and activities related to how an organization checks and tests artifacts produced throughout the software development lifecycle. This typically includes quality assurance work, such as testing, but it can also include other review and evaluation activities.

Deployment entails the processes and activities related to how an organization manages the release of software that has been created. This can involve shipping products to end users, deploying products to internal or external hosts, and normal operations of software in the runtime environment.

Two security practices that are most pertinent to the focus areas of this book will be described in detail. These two security practices are a:

- *Security Requirements* from *Construction*
- *Security Testing* from *Verification*

10.2   Security Requirements

The Security Requirements (SR) Practice is focused on proactively specifying the expected behavior of software with respect to security. Through the addition of analysis activities at the project level, security requirements are initially gathered based on the high-level business purpose of the software. As an organization advances, more advanced techniques, such as access control specifications, are used to discover new security requirements that may not have been initially obvious to development.

The key objectives, activities, assessment, and expected results for each of the maturity levels for Security Requirements are summarized in Figure 10.2.

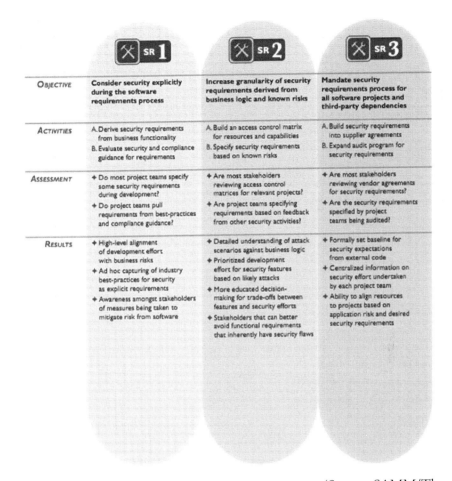

	SR 1	SR 2	SR 3
OBJECTIVE	Consider security explicitly during the software requirements process	Increase granularity of security requirements derived from business logic and known risks	Mandate security requirements process for all software projects and third-party dependencies
ACTIVITIES	A. Derive security requirements from business functionality B. Evaluate security and compliance guidance for requirements	A. Build an access control matrix for resources and capabilities B. Specify security requirements based on known risks	A. Build security requirements into supplier agreements B. Expand audit program for security requirements
ASSESSMENT	✦ Do most project teams specify some security requirements during development? ✦ Do project teams pull requirements from best-practices and compliance guidance?	✦ Are most stakeholders reviewing access control matrices for relevant projects? ✦ Are project teams specifying requirements based on feedback from other security activities?	✦ Are most stakeholders reviewing vendor agreements for security requirements? ✦ Are the security requirements specified by project teams being audited?
RESULTS	✦ High-level alignment of development effort with business risks ✦ Ad hoc capturing of industry best-practices for security as explicit requirements ✦ Awareness amongst stakeholders of measures being taken to mitigate risk from software	✦ Detailed understanding of attack scenarios against business logic ✦ Prioritized development effort for security features based on likely attacks ✦ More educated decision-making for trade-offs between features and security efforts ✦ Stakeholders that can better avoid functional requirements that inherently have security flaws	✦ Formally set baseline for security expectations from external code ✦ Centralized information on security effort undertaken by each project team ✦ Ability to align resources to projects based on application risk and desired security requirements

Figure 10.2   OpenSAMM–Security Requirements Practice (Source: SAMM/The Security Practices, p. 50)

10.2.1   Security Requirements: Level 1

Level 1 is the first level of maturity of this security practice, referred to as SR1. The objective here is to consider security explicitly during the software requirements process.

SR1: Activities

Two activities are listed for SR1:

A. Derive Security Requirements from Business Functionality

Conduct a review of functional requirements that specify the business logic and overall behavior for each software project. After gathering requirements for a project, conduct an assessment to derive relevant security requirements. Even if software is being built by a third party, these requirements, once identified, should be included with functional requirements delivered to vendors.

For each functional requirement, a security auditor should lead stakeholders through the process of explicitly noting any expectations with regard to security. Typically, questions to clarify for each requirement include expectations for data security, access control, transaction integrity, criticality of business function, separation of duties, uptime, and the like.

It is important to ensure that all security requirements follow the same principles for writing good requirements in general. Specifically, they should be specific, measurable, and reasonable.

Conduct this process for all new requirements on active projects. For existing features, it is recommended to conduct the same process as a gap analysis to fuel future refactoring for security.

B. Evaluate Security and Compliance Guidance for Requirements

Identify industry best practices that project teams should treat as requirements. These can be chosen from publicly available guidelines, internal or external guidelines/standards/policies, or established compliance requirements.

It is important to not attempt to bring too many best-practice requirements into each development iteration, since there is a time tradeoff with design and implementation. The recommended approach is to slowly add best practices over successive development cycles to bolster the software's overall assurance profile over time.

For existing systems, refactoring for security best practices can be a complex undertaking. Where possible, add security requirements opportunistically when adding new features. At a minimum, the analysis should be conducted in such a way as to identify applicable best practices to help fuel future planning efforts.

This review should be performed by a security auditor with input from business stakeholders. Senior developers, architects, and other technical stakeholders should also be involved to bring design and implementation-specific knowledge into the decision process.

SR1: Results

The results or outcomes from achieving maturity-level SR1 include:

- A high-level alignment of development effort with business risks
- Ad hoc capturing of industry best practices for security as explicit requirements
- Awareness among stakeholders of measures that are being taken to mitigate risks from software

10.2.2   Security Requirements: Level 2

The second level of maturity security requirements practice is referred to as SR2. The objective is to increase the granularity of security requirements derived from business logic and known risks.

SR2: Activities

Two activities are listed for SR2:

A. Build an Access Control Matrix for Resources and Capabilities

Based upon the business purpose of the application, identify user and operator roles. Additionally, build a list of resources and capabilities by gathering all relevant data assets and application-specific features that are guarded by any form of access control.

In a simple matrix with roles on one axis and resources on the other, consider the relationships between each role and each resource, and note in each intersection the correct behavior of the system in terms of access control according to stakeholders.

For data resources, it is important to note access rights in terms of creation, read access, update, and deletion (CRUD). For resources that are features, gradation of access rights will likely be application-specific, but at a minimum note whether the role should be permitted access to the feature.

This permission matrix will serve as an artifact to document the correct access control rights for the business logic of the overall system. As such, it should be created by the project teams with input from business stakeholders. After initial creation, it should be updated by business stakeholders before every release, but usually toward the beginning of the design phase.

B. Specify Security Requirements Based on Known Risks
Explicitly review existing artifacts that indicate organization- or project-specific security risk to better understand the overall risk profile for the software. When available, draw on resources such as the high-level business risk profile, individual application threat models, findings from design review, code review, security testing, and the like.

In addition to review of existing artifacts, use abuse-case models for an application to serve as fuel for identification of concrete security requirements that directly or indirectly mitigate the abuse scenarios.

This process should be conducted by business owners and security auditors as needed. Ultimately, the notion of risks leading to new security requirements should become a built-in step in the planning phase, whereby newly discovered risks are specifically assessed by project teams.

SR2: Results

The outcomes from achieving maturity-level SR2 include:

- A detailed understanding of attack scenarios against business logic
- Prioritized development efforts for security features based on likely attacks
- Better-educated decision making for tradeoffs between features and security efforts
- Stakeholders who can better avoid functional requirements that are inherently flawed with security vulnerabilities.

10.2.3   Security Requirements: Level 3

The third level of maturity of practice is referred to as SR3. The objective is to *mandate* a security requirements process for all software projects and third-party dependencies.

SR3: Activities

Two activities are listed for SR3:

A. Build Security Requirements into Supplier Agreements
Beyond the kinds of security requirements already identified by previous analysis, additional security benefits can be derived from third-party agreements. Typically, requirements and perhaps high-level design will be developed internally, while detailed design and implementation is often left up to suppliers.

Based on the specific division of labor for each externally developed component, identify specific security activities and technical assessment criteria to add to the vendor contracts. Commonly, this is a set of activities from the Design Review, Code Review, and Security Testing Practices.

Modifications of agreement language should be handled on a case-by-case basis with each supplier, since adding additional requirements will generally mean an increase in cost. The cost of each potential security activity should be balanced against the benefit of the activity as per the usage of the component or system being considered.

B. Expand the Audit Program for Security Requirements

Incorporate checks for completeness of security requirements into routine project audits. Since this can be difficult to gauge without project-specific knowledge, the audit should focus on checking project artifacts such as requirements or design documentation for evidence that the proper types of analysis were conducted.

Particularly, each functional requirement should be annotated with security requirements based on business drivers as well as expected abuse scenarios. The overall project requirements should contain a list of requirements generated from best practices in guidelines and standards. Additionally, there should be a clear list of unfulfilled security requirements and an estimated timeline for their provision in future releases.

This audit should be performed during every development iteration, ideally toward the end of the requirements process, but it must be performed before a release can be made.

SR3: Results

The results from achieving maturity-level SR3 include:

- A formally set baseline for security expectations from external code
- Centralized information about software security efforts undertaken by each project team
- An ability to align resources to projects based on application risk and desired security requirements

10.3   Security Testing

Security Testing involves testing the organization's software in its runtime environment in order to both discover vulnerabilities and establish a minimum standard for software releases.

The Security Testing Practice is focused on inspection of software in the runtime environment to find security problems. These testing activities bolster the assurance case for software by checking it in the same context in which it is expected to run, thus making visible operational misconfigurations or errors in business logic that are difficult to otherwise find.

Starting with penetration testing and high-level test cases based on the functionality of software, an organization evolves toward usage of security testing automation to cover the wide variety of test cases that might demonstrate vulnerability in the system.

The key objectives, activities, assessment and expected results for each of the maturity levels for Security Testing are summarized in Figure 10.3.

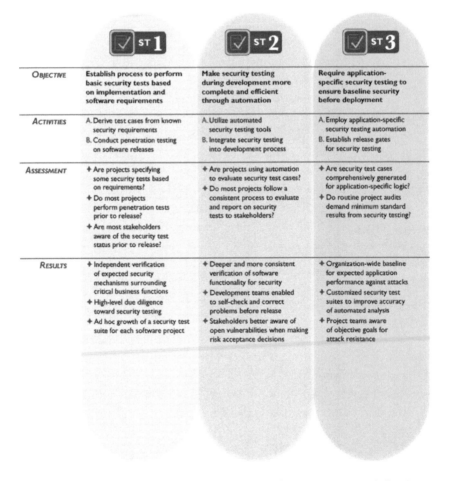

Figure 10.3   OpenSAMM–Security Testing Practice (Source: SAMM/The Security Practices, p. 66)

10.3.1   Security Testing: Level 1

Level 1 is first level of maturity of the Security Testing practice and is referred to as ST1. The objective is to establish processes to perform basic security tests based on implementation and software requirements.

ST1: Activities
ST1 consists of two activities:

A. Derive Test Cases from Known Security Requirements
From the known security requirements for a project, identify a set of test cases to check the software for correct functionality. Typically, these test cases are derived from security concerns surrounding the functional requirements and business logic of the system, but should also include generic tests for common vulnerabilities based on the implementation language or technology stack.

Often, it is most effective to use the project team's time to build application-specific test cases and use publicly available resources or purchased knowledge bases to select applicable general test cases for security. Although they are not required, automated security testing tools can also be used to cover the general security test cases.

This test case planning should occur during the requirements and/or design phases, but must occur before final testing prior to release. Candidate test cases should be reviewed for applicability, efficacy, and feasibility by relevant development, security, and quality assurance staff.

B. Conduct Penetration Testing on Software Releases
Using the set of security test cases identified for each project, penetration testing should be conducted to evaluate the system's performance against each case. It is common for this to occur during the testing phase prior to release.

Penetration testing cases should include both application-specific tests to check soundness of business logic as well as common vulnerability tests to check the design and implementation. Once specified, security test cases can be executed by security-savvy quality assurance or development staff, but first-time execution of security test cases for a project team should be monitored by a security auditor to assist and coach team members.

Prior to release or deployment, stakeholders must review results of security tests and accept the risks indicated by failing security tests at release time. In the latter case, a concrete timeline should be established to address the gaps over time.

ST1: Results

The results or outcomes from achieving maturity-level ST1 include:

- Independent verification of expected security mechanisms surrounding critical business functions
- High-level due diligence toward security testing
- Ad hoc growth of a security test suite for each software project

10.3.2   Security Testing: Level 2

ST2 is second level of maturity of security testing practice. The objective is to improve security testing during the development stage by making it more complete and efficient through automation.

ST2: Activities

The two activities in ST2 include:

A. Use Automated Security Testing Tools

To test for security issues, a potentially large number of input cases must be checked against each software interface, which can make effective security testing using manual test case implementation and execution unwieldy. Thus, automated security test tools should be used to automatically test software, resulting in more efficient security testing and higher quality results.

Both commercial and open-source products are available and should be reviewed for appropriateness for the organization. Selecting a a suitable tool is based on several factors, including robustness and accuracy of built-in security test cases, efficacy at testing architecture types important to organization, customization to change or add test cases, quality and usability of findings to the development organization, and the like.

Use input from security-savvy technical staff as well as development and quality assurance staff in the selection process, and review overall results with stakeholders.

B. Integrate Security Testing into Development Process

With tools to run automated security tests, projects within the organization should routinely run security tests and review results during development. To make this scalable with low overhead, security testing tools should be configured to automatically run on a routine basis (e.g., nightly or weekly) and findings should be inspected as they occur.

Conducting security tests as early as the requirements or design phases can be beneficial. While traditionally, used for functional test cases, this type of test-driven development approach involves identifying and running relevant security test cases early in the development cycle, usually during design. With the automatic execution of security test cases, projects enter the implementation phase with a number of failing tests for the nonexistent functionality. Implementation is complete when all the tests pass. This provides a clear, upfront goal for developers early in the development cycle, thus lowering the risk of release delays due to security concerns or the forced acceptance of risk to meet project deadlines.

For each project release, results from automated and manual security tests should be presented to management and business stakeholders for review. If there are unaddressed findings that remain as accepted risks for the release, stakeholders and development managers should work together to establish a concrete timeframe for addressing them.

ST2: Results

The results that can be expected from ST2 maturity include:

- A deeper and more consistent verification of software functionality for security
- Development teams that are enabled to self-check and correct problems before release
- Stakeholders who are better aware of open vulnerabilities when making risk acceptance decisions

10.3.3   Security Testing: Level 3

Security Testing Level 3 is the third level of maturity of the Security Testing practice and is referred to as ST3. The objective is to require application-specific security testing to ensure baseline security before deployment.

ST3: Activities

The two activities within ST3 are:

A. Employ Application-Specific Security Testing Automation

Through customization of security testing tools, enhancements to generic test case execution tools, or build-out of custom test harnesses, project teams should formally iterate through security requirements and build a set of automated checkers to test the security of the implemented business logic.

Additionally, many automated security testing tools can be greatly improved in accuracy and depth of coverage if they are customized to understand more detail about the specific software interfaces in the project under test. Further, organization-specific concerns from compliance or technical standards can be codified as a reusable, central test battery to make audit data collection and per-project management visibility simpler.

Project teams should focus on build-out of granular security test cases based on the business functionality of their software, and an organization-level team led by a security auditor should focus on specification of automated tests for compliance and internal standards.

B. Establish Release Gates for Security Testing

To prevent software from being released with easily found security bugs, a particular point in the software development lifecycle should be identified as a checkpoint that an established set of security test cases must pass in order to make a release from the project. This establishes a baseline for the kinds of security tests all projects are expected to pass.

Since adding too many test cases initially can result in an overhead cost bubble, begin by choosing one or two security issues and include a wide variety of test cases for each, with the expectation that no project may pass if any test fails. Over time, this baseline should be improved by selecting additional security issues and adding a variety of corresponding test cases.

Generally, this security testing checkpoint should occur toward the end of the implementation or testing, but must occur before release.

For legacy systems or inactive projects, an exception process should be created to allow those projects to continue operations, but with an explicitly assigned timeframe for mitigation of findings. Exceptions should be limited to no more that 20 percent of all projects.

ST3: Results

Results that are expected from achieving ST3 maturity include:

- Organization-wide baselines for expected application performance against attacks
- Customized security test suites to improve accuracy of automated analysis
- Project teams who are aware of objective goals for attack resistance

10.4   Wrap-Up

You've seen throughout the book what it takes to *genuinely* secure applications that you build for yourself, your customers, your partners, as well as what it takes to operate them to maintain their security and resilience. What we hope to achieve with this book is to provide you with resources that are proven to work while we ease the effort and fear of making wide-sweeping changes in how software is developed. We hope you've come to understand that building security and resilience into application software is the *only way* it will get in there–bolting in on afterward will never succeed as a strategy or a tactic.

Building security in is akin to baking. Should you forget, for example, the eggs when you bake a cake, you won't be able to add them once the cake comes out of the oven. The activities and effort you expend on securing software while it's in process will spare you from the pain and agony you'll most certainly experience when your applications are targeted and breached.

Oh, and don't forget the eggs!

10.5   References

1. *Software Assurance Maturity Model*, www.opensamm.org, retrieved June 5, 2011, http://www.opensamm.org/downloads/ SAMM-1.0-en_US.pdf

Index

Printed and bound by CPI Group (UK) Ltd, Croydon, CR0 4YY

23/10/2024

01777673-0008